preted the language of biblical prophecy, a subject that Coleridge studied in the work of Sir Isaac Newton.

In most of Coleridge's best poems one or both of the two kinds of symbolism are present. The symbolism of nature is in the foreground of the Conversation Poems where the most common theme is the discovery of God in nature and the implications of that discovery for the moral life. In the supernatural poems the symbolism, of both kinds, subsumes the prose meaning and relates it to the theme of love, of the joy that is a release from isolation, guilt, and despair.

In the last two chapters, Piper discusses the changes brought about by Coleridge's attraction to German idealist philosophy as expressed in the "Letter to Asra," his influence on the symbolism of the other Romantic poets, and finally his continued adherence to his belief in the inspired symbolism of nature and the Bible and his use of transcendental theories of symbolism in the defense of religion.

This study offers much new material on the sources of Coleridge's symbolism, as well as a new perspective on the religious nature of his quest for joy.

D0875195

The
Singing
of Mount Abora

The
Singing
of Mount Abora

Coleridge's Use of Biblical Imagery and Natural Symbolism in Poetry and Philosophy

H. W. Piper

Rutherford ● Madison ● Teaneck
Fairleigh Dickinson University Press
London and Toronto: Associated University Presses

Associated University Presses
440 Forsgate Drive
Cranbury, NJ 08512

Associated University Presses
25 Sicilian Avenue
London WC1A 2QH, England

Associated University Presses
2133 Royal Windsor Drive
Unit 1
Mississauga, Ontario
Canada L5J 1K5

Some parts of this study have appeared, in earlier forms, in *The Review of
English Studies, Essays in Criticism,* and *Southern Review* (Adelaide).
I wish to thank Doctor Elizabeth Liggins for her careful reading of my man-
uscript.

Library of Congress Cataloging-in-Publication Data

Piper, H. W. (Herbert Walter), 1915–
  The singing of Mount Abora.

  Bibliography: p.
  Includes index.
  1. Coleridge, Samuel Taylor, 1772–1834—Symbolism.
  2. Coleridge, Samuel Taylor, 1772–1834—Religion.
  3. Symbolism in literature.   4. Bible in literature.
  5. Nature in literature.   I. Title.
  PR4487.S95P56   1987   821'.7   86-45480
  ISBN 0-8386-3295-5 (alk. paper)

Printed in the United States of America

Ad Manes
J. A. W. Bennett
C. S. Lewis

Contents

Preface

This book is an attempt to throw fresh light on Coleridge's more important poems by examining his interest in symbolism and in biblical imagery, both in idea and as they emerged in his poetry. It was an interest which lasted from the time he left Cambridge at the end of 1794 to embark on the career of a poet and preacher, continued through his period as a major poet, and finally played some part in his later work as a religious apologist. (There is a certain continuity in his religious thinking despite the well-known changes of allegiance.)

One consequence of the importance to Coleridge of religious ideas is that the vividness and strangeness of the imagery in his most important poems are not the accidental result of miscellaneous reading, as it is sometimes thought to be. Rather this imagery, like the equally strange and vivid (though different) imagery of Blake, had its origin in the poet's commitment to extreme and radically nonconformist religion, a commitment that for Coleridge lasted until the early years of the nineteenth century. Coleridge's lifelong faith that nature and the Bible were two forms of the Word of God took various formulations, but it had its origin in the faith he adopted in 1794, which reconciled for him two seemingly disparate elements, being biblical and millenarian in that it saw the French Revolution as the beginning of the Last Days prophesied in the Bible, while it was rational and "scientific" in that it sought the foundations of religious experience in psychology (that of Hartley) and in that it found God in Nature. Oddly, it was this latter aspect that led Coleridge, in his Nature poems, to at least the edge of the kind of mysticism that is to be found in the early Wordsworth, while the first aspect led to a way of seeing human feelings that produced, amid all the supernatural romanticism of his strangest poems, the powerful and subtle treatment of emotion in the "human interest," though both aspects of his religion must have worked together.

Though Coleridge learned the importance of both natural and biblical symbolism (even if he would at that time have called the latter "prophetic

9

language") from his religious mentors and, in the case of natural symbolism, from the eighteenth-century "nature" poets, yet he early developed the use of both, and the range of possible meanings in them, in his poetry. In his nature poetry his sense of the life of God in natural scenes and objects led him to a more immediate sense of moral implication and thence into religious ecstasy. At about the same time he began to see the figures of the "prophetic language" as referring to states of mind and religious attitudes rather than to physical events. There is nothing specifically nonconformist about this: the kingdom of heaven is always within and in the Christian tradition the biblical descriptions of paradise and hell have always been known to be symbolical, and even the Unitarian leader Joseph Priestley treated the millennium as such a description of heaven on earth, brought about by Christian love. Nevertheless, the interest in psychology that David Hartley sparked in Coleridge continued through his life, and he was able to use the biblical imagery to trace complex states of feeling.

Thus for Coleridge, from 1794 religious faith was based on the mind—not the mind as a rational instrument or a philosophical concept but as a complex of thought and feeling—and, as always in the central Christian tradition, religion itself was an affair of feelings and states of mind. The interest of such states is not confined to religious contexts only: what the religious symbolism offers is a way of describing a number of fundamental human feelings: despair, isolation, joy, love, fear, agony, guilt (as a feeling, not as an objective condition), and release. The biblical imagery carries these feelings in ways that can be, and in Coleridge's major poetry are, independent of religious categories, and, though Coleridge learned from the "prophetic language," it was developed in the poems from his own psychological and introspective thought.

Thus Coleridge was, in the 1790s, in possession of two traditions of religious symbolism, both concerned with important states of mind. The first, which came to him both as a believer in God's presence in nature and as heir to later eighteenth-century nature poetry, was that the beautiful forms of nature were symbols of God and that his qualities could be read in the emotional reaction to landscapes: one aspect of his poems, and particularly of what have become known as the Conversation Poems, deals with the ecstasy of discovering God in the beauty of the forms of nature, and it is this ecstasy which sometimes approaches mysticism. The other tradition was that which interpreted the language of biblical prophecy, a subject that Coleridge studied in the work of Sir Isaac Newton, who gave a great deal of his energy to the subject, even if his interpretations were more often mechanical and political than spiritual (though the prophecies of Ezekiel and Saint John have always had interpreters, from Origen to Swedenborg and beyond, who looked more deeply). In Coleridge's earlier poems he usually employed the prophetic language politically, but when the imagery emerged more freely in later poems, particularly In *Kubla Khan* and *The Ancient Mariner,* it was to carry Coleridge's poetic thought about human feeling and states of mind.

These images or symbols are worth pursuing both for their importance as an expression, and as a medium, for Coleridge's thought and for the light they cast on the poems. Of course, the identification of this kind of symbolism does not alter the effect of the poems, just as, in Shakespeare, the finding of symbolic values in the settings of Belmont and the Rialto in *The Merchant of Venice* or of Egypt and Rome in *Antony and Cleopatra* clarifies rather than alters our understanding of those plays. The effect of the work (though perhaps without the same clarity) can be got intuitively by sensitive readers, as we can see in the case of *Kubla Khan,* where many critics have recognized that the poem is about joy but have then gone on to argue about whether the root of that joy was poetry or sex or energy or whatever, without recognizing that in this tradition a poem about paradise is a symbolic discussion of joy itself. Certainly for most of Coleridge's best poems, a knowledge of the symbolism is worth having, and in these we can usually say confidently what symbols are being used, because they are ones which Coleridge himself acknowledged earlier, either under the name of symbol or "prophetic language," and which he had used either individually or typically (in less powerful ways) in earlier poems.

In most of Coleridge's best poems one or both of the two kinds of symbolism are present. The symbolism of nature is in the foreground of the Conversation Poems where the most common theme is the discovery of God in nature and the implications of that discovery for the moral life. (Clearly, if Wordsworth was a mystic, Coleridge was at least a mystic manqué, knowing the understanding that such an ecstasy should bring, but perhaps never quite reaching that understanding himself.) In the supernatural poems the symbolism, of both kinds, subsumes the prose meaning and relates it to the themes of love, of the joy that is a release from isolation, guilt, and despair. A meditation carried on in terms of symbolism cannot be as clear-cut as a logical discussion but it can suggest relations the other cannot. Its province is that of the feelings and of those reasons that the reason cannot know. The poet has done his thinking as a poet and found poetical and emotional resolution in his handling of the symbols. It is for the scholar to offer what paraphrase may be possible.

Coleridge's interest in symbolism did not end with his poetry. He once asked Godwin "the old (question), 'Is Logic the *Essence* of Thinking?' in other words—Is *thinking* impossible without arbitrary signs, &—how far is the word 'arbitrary' a misnomer?"[1] Without going into the question of logic, it can be said that much, perhaps most, religious thinking has taken place in terms of metaphor, allegory, and parable. To quote Coleridge again, "What the Spirit of God *is* and what the Soul *is* . . .are *known* by those, to whom they are revealed. . . . They can only be explained by images."[2] So, when he turned almost wholly to philosophy, some part of his effort was given to trying to use ideas of symbolism, under the guidance of the German idealist philosophers, for the purposes of religious understanding. It was an ambitious effort, involving *Naturphilosophie* and natural symbolism, and it was overall a failure, but there were other dealings with symbolism where Coleridge struck out for himself. Perhaps the original attraction of German philosophy for Coleridge was its attempt to deduce religious faith not from historical evidences but from the very nature of the human mind: he once quoted "St Paul's assertion that the Spirit of God bears witness to the spirit of man,"[3] and he could perhaps have said reasonably that the inverse was also true. This meant an approach through the symbol-making powers of the human mind, and in *The Statesman's Manual* and some other later writings he made this approach not through *Naturphilosophie* but through the symbolism which he had long known and which could be approached more easily—the human responses to the book of Holy Writ and the book of nature. How far that evidence still touches one is a matter of individual and personal concern, but to follow Coleridge here is to know him a little better as a poet and a thinker. The language of Scripture and the forms of nature were two forms of symbolism that concerned him when he first left Cambridge and began to think seriously for himself: together they formed an intellectual path which he trod all his life and along which it is the purpose of this study to track him.

The
Singing
of Mount Abora

1
Symbolism and Coleridge's Religion

COLERIDGE stands at an interesting position in the history of literary symbolism. He reaches forward, through his influence on Edgar Allan Poe, to the French Symbolist poets of the nineteenth century; he concerned himself throughout his literary life with ideas about the nature of symbolism, and he himself introduced new forms of symbolism into the romantic movement. At the same time, because his interest in symbolism was developed as part of his religious thought and feeling, he reached back to a tradition of biblical symbolism elaborated by the medievals from that of the Hebrew prophets, and he transmuted this in his poetry. The religious aspect of the symbolism is not immediately apparent in his major poems because these are most immediately in terms of emotion, not theology: Coleridge's religion placed great emphasis on religious psychology (Hartley's system of psychology was very important in it) and his greatest poems deal with states of mind. Nevertheless these emotions are still in essence religious: joy, despair, the apprehension of the divine in the world, and the feelings aroused in the attempt to reconcile this with the sense of evil in the same world. Indeed, his greatest poems gain much of their force from the fact that so much of their imagery took its rise in religious symbolism designed to express just such feelings.

Since the use of the word "symbolism" in literary applications dates only from the end of the eighteenth century, the biblical language concerned would have been described before then as allegorical or anagogical and the word "symbol" would have meant a *thing* standing for something else, like a cross or crescent or alphabetical letter: it is necessary therefore to look carefully at the literary meaning of the word. Even among literary critics there are a number of technical definitions belonging to anthropological or psychological theories (which are not helpful in criticism) but in broad literary use the word indicates a metaphor that is marked by great complexity of meaning and does not so much define as suggest. The "meaning" is the product of all the implications that can be drawn from the metaphor, or set of metaphors, and the less it is tied to immediate reference the more complex these implications can become. But the most important element of a literary symbol is the feeling, and it is even more than usually wrong to separate meaning and feeling here.

The French Symbolist poets of the nineteenth century used complex symbols as independent free-standing structures constituting the whole poem, but other poets, earlier or later, have always been given to using such complex structures of metaphor to support their lyrics or dramas or narratives. Thus, for example, in *Antony and Cleopatra* there is a continuous recurrence of Egypt with metaphoric reference to its fertility, its riches, its strangeness, its worship of a female divinity in Isis, and even to the idea that its inhabitants are gypsies, all of which serves both to enlarge and to define Cleopatra's part in the relationship with Antony, as well as to enlarge and to define the emotions the audience feels towards her.

The symbolism here is based on a view of Egypt and its gypies already found in tradition. More commonly in more recent poetry there is a formal symbolic scheme. When Yeats interrogated the spirits who provided the material for *A Vision*, they disclaimed any intention of providing universal truths: "No," was the answer, "we have come to give you metaphors for poetry."[1]

Nevertheless they did provide a system that made the meaning of the metaphors clear. Coleridge provided no such system, and indeed, he did his best to suggest that these poems had no coherence at all and no purpose beyond entertainment. He published *Kubla Khan* as a psychological curiosity and he insisted that *The Ancient Mariner* should be taken on the same terms as the Arabian Nights story of the punishment of the traveller who accidentally blinded a completely invisible Genie, while (apart from one interesting remark) he dealt with the complexity of feeling in *Christabel* by suggesting several different but equally vapid endings to the narrative. What is common to such explanations is their evasiveness. Poetry of this power and resonance is not frivolous. It does not spring simply from miscellaneous reading, nor can opium put into the mind anything that was not already there, much less shape it as these poems are shaped, nor are great poems ever purely or merely literary. Great poetry does not come from the shallows of human experience.

Coleridge's brilliance, his mercurial temperament, and the elusiveness and self-doubt that were part of his character have made it easy to regard him as a kind of prodigy fallen from the clouds, whose work has something to say to our imaginations but little to our lives. His major poems are sometimes thought of as pure fantasies, or as being about literary interests and hence rooted in reading rather than life, in much the same way as his later life was concerned with points of philosophy. In fact, all his letters and notebooks show, in remark after remark, that the continuing and important interest of his life was not his poetry, nor his philosophising, nor his loves, but his religious life. The poetical ambitions of Coleridge's early years and the philosophical ambitions of his later ones were in origin essentially religious: he saw himself first as the poet of a purer belief in Christianity and then as the defender of a more philosophical one. Of course, the poetry of Coleridge's *annus mirabilis*, 1797–98, is not normally religious in any overt or doctrinaire way, as his poetry of only one year earlier had been, but it would be a very limiting mistake to regard his major poems as purely literary—to think that *Kubla Khan* is about the writing of poetry, or that *The Ancient Mariner* is a dream world of traveler's tales, or *Christabel* just a Gothic romance. The emotional states which these capture had their roots in his religious experience and the literary methods which capture them were also developed from religious ideas: not the least of Coleridge's contributions to English romantic poetry was his transformation of older religious symbolism into poetic symbolism. The major poems of 1797–98 are not versified sermons and they are not concerned with discursive reason but with feeling, but the feelings are those of a man whose thinking was religious.

This dimension of his poetry is not always remembered, perhaps because his earlier beliefs are often regarded with contempt or ignored. Scholars have said some very crass things about them: statements that Coleridge did not write as a Christian before 1817 or that his poetry of the 1790s contained "cheerful godlessness" are as absurd as statements that in 1795 he was "an orthodox Christian" or that he was at that time interested in the defense of the Established Church.[2] In fact he was a Unitarian preacher (though not a paid one) until his visit to Germany in 1798–99 and, though dissatisfied with some aspects of Unitarianism after that (certainly its Hartleyanism), he remained at least a "Negative Unitarian," that is to say a man who, though he had abandoned the metaphysical system of Hartley and Priestley, with its base in the passivity of the mind, still shared the Unitarians' belief in the impersonality of the Deity and their scheme of morality (though he had always had his own opinion on certain points)[3]—until his visit to Malta in 1805. Until then he was strongly opposed to the Anglican church, to Trinitarianism, to the doctrine that Christ's suffering and death were necessary to appease God's wrath (though, as Robert Barth, S. J., explains, this particular way of explaining Christ's sacrifice is not the only patristic one)[4] and to the sacrament of the Lord's Supper, which was supposed to commemorate this, but he was always a Christian, however heretical, and his religion in the 1790s was strongly biblical as well as strongly philosophical. It was to him a rational faith held with moral fervor.

If only because it was Coleridge's faith in his poetically creative years, eighteenth-century Unitarianism needs to be better known to his readers.[5] The account of this Unitarianism most available to Coleridgeans would be Basil Willey's chapter in his *Eighteenth Century Background*.[6] This gives a good account of Joseph Priestley, the chief Unitarian theological writer of the period, but it has less to say about the Unitarian church. This was, in effect, the English Presbyterian church with a metamorphosis of doctrine, a church of considerable solidity both intellectually and socially.[7] One of Willey's great strengths in writing of the later Coleridge is his own deep commitment to Trinitarianism, but this does not make for a sympathetic treatment of Coleridge's faith in his vital poetic years, which Willey treats rather as a philosophy than as a religion. Willey assumes, reasonably enough from his religious viewpoint, that the Scriptures are plainly Trinitarian and that the Unitarians, giving their first allegiance to rationalism, had to produce ingenious arguments to get around the texts.[8] In fact, the Unitarians reached their beliefs, whether these be right or wrong, by an examination of Scripture texts without recourse to tradition, and for them reason was only a tool in this. (Priestley provided philosophical defenses but this was *post hoc*.) In the nineteenth century James Martineau wrote:

> There is one unorthodox influence so powerful and so extensively diffused as almost to supersede inquiry into the pedigree of English Unitarianism—I mean the English Bible. . . . The earlier Unitarians, notwithstanding their repute as rationalists, drew their doctrine out of the Scriptures, much to their own surprise, and did not import it into them.[9]

That interest in Scripture was important to Coleridge, even as a poet.

The other aspect of Willey's treatment which might seem unsatisfactory to someone looking for formative influences on a young poet is the description of Unitarianism as an almost purely philosophical and rationalistic faith, a description that is at least inadequate for the millenarian church, with its expectation of the apocalypse and with the thirst for righteousness and social justice in which it rivaled the Evangelicals (whose work it seconded in the abolition of the slave trade and the passage of the Factory Acts). Certainly Coleridge after his return from Germany described Socinianism as "moonlight," with its implication of a cold and faint rationality, but anyone who reads the early poems in which Coleridge set out his Unitarian faith will find bombast and turgidity in plenty, but not faintness nor coldness, let alone excessive rationality.

There were Unitarian churches in Europe during the sixteenth and seventeenth centuries with Sozzini (Socinus) as their chief theologian, but in England it remained a forbidden doctrine until the arrival of toleration, and there were executions for Unitarianism as late as 1612 in England and 1697 in Scotland. In the eighteenth century Milton was suspected, and Sir Isaac Newton was known, to have been Unitarian,[10] but the development of English Unitarianism as a church was a slow process which began in English Presbyterianism after its disestablishment in 1662 and culminated in the wholesale transfer of Presbyterian congregations to Unitarianism after the mid-eighteenth century. The process has been described as follows:

> The English Presbyterians first admitted the essential value of human good works and from this concession the acknowledgement of the authority of the reason and the right of the individual to interpret the Scriptures for himself logically followed. Having accepted these principles, the Presbyterians became converted to Arianism, which seemed to conform more closely than the Trinitarian doctrine both to the text and the dictates of reason. Finally they rejected Arianism on account of the confused arguments, which involved a multiplicity of ideal forms, and adopted Socinianism, which appeared to them the only form of Christian faith which harmonized with the Necessitarianism and Materialism which they believed scientific research had absolutely established.[11]

Arianism is the doctrine that Christ is quasi-divine and pre-existent but that he was not eternal and that he is inferior to God the Father.

It will be seen from this account that reason, though of great importance, comes after Scripture in authority and only produces dogma when it is applied to Scripture. Even the materialism comes from the Unitarian belief that, in the Bible, resurrection is always resurrection of the whole man. The important first step in the chain of reason just described came in 1719 at the Salters Hall synod of Presbyterians, Independents, and Baptists, who adopted the doctrine of the sufficiency of Scripture by a small majority. (The presiding officer announced, "The Bible has it by four.") Most of the majority were Presbyterians and they now proceeded to apply the doctrine wholeheartedly to the text, without considering tradition or traditional doctrine. They were struck by the number of texts that seem to imply that the Son is inferior to the Father, an important tenet of Arianism. But further, the application of reason to Scripture included its application to textual matters, and the Presbyterians decided that the text of 1 John 5:7 ("For there are three that bear witness in Heaven.") was spurious, an interpolation based on Trinitarian doctrine rather than a support for it (the text not being found in early manuscripts) and in this they were supported by Porson, the leading textual scholar of his era. Coleridge's early interest in Michaelis, the pioneer of biblical higher criticism, was typically Unitarian, and so too was his general interest in such criticism.[12] The movement from Arianism to Unitarianism can be seen in the resolution of 1753 by the Exeter Assembly that candidates might be admitted to ordination without declaring their faith in the divinity of the Son or of the Holy Spirit,[13] and at this time the dissenting acadamies, which were the nonconformist substitute for Oxford and Cambridge, but which did not require any attestation of doctrine, had on their staffs a number of Unitarians (and Arians). In 1752, a year earlier than the Exeter Assembly, Joseph Priestley became a student at Daventry Academy, where he became an Arian, came under the influence of the psychology of David Hartley, and began his career as a religious apologist.

Priestley is now best known as the discoverer of oxygen but he was also an indefatigable thinker and writer on subjects ranging from grammar to electricity. The bulk of his writing was philosophical and theological, and, after he took the step from Arianism to Unitarianism in 1767, his greatest efforts were aimed at the development and defense of Unitarianism. (For some years he published an annual defense of Unitarianism.) What Priestley propagated was a coherent body of Socinian doctrine, for the application of human reason to text and doctrine took its followers into many other beliefs beside the Unitarian nature of God (and, indeed, Unitarians sometimes objected to the name as concentrating attention on a single, if important, element in their faith). Though the subscription of belief required by the Unitarian congregations was very simple, yet the writings of Priestley show that he, and those for whom he was the spokesman, came to the same conclusions as Socinus on many other matters. Certainly Coleridge did. These other beliefs included many that Coleridge held right up to his conversion to orthodoxy—for instance, an opposition to the orthodox idea that Christ's sacrifice on the Cross was a sacrifice to God the Father to atone for man's sins. For Unitarians the central point of the Gospel story was rather the Resurrection, and Christ had been chosen by God to receive the eternal life that he would eventually offer to all men. Another point of difference was eternal damnation. Socinians believed that God would eventually admit all men to eternal happiness, and they disliked the orthodox Calvinist doctrine that a large part of mankind had been predestined by God to eternal and necessary damnation. Even when he had been converted to Trinitarianism, it seems (as will appear later) to have taken Coleridge a very long time to reconcile himself to these doctrines.

One of Priestley's most important services to Unitarianism was to produce a scientific theory of materialism that reconciled matter to spirit. Priestley took up the theory of the Italian Father Boscovitch, whose ideas represented the first stirring of what has become the ordinary view of matter—that it is a form of energy. (His theory remained scientifically very respectable until the rise of Dalton and became again so with the rise of modern physics.) Boscovitch argued that the qualities which matter had been given in Newton's mechanics, particularly solidity, were merely the apparent effects of this energy, solidity being merely resistance. For Priestley matter as energy was the same thing as spirit as energy, and complete materialism was only another word for complete spiritualism. To this system Priestley added an idea of Giordano Bruno's—that all this energy was finally the divine energy of God acting throughout the universe. Priestley allowed the existence of subordinate intelligences, such as those of men, but these were acted upon by, and acted as parts of, this chain of divine energy. This system meant that he (and Coleridge following him) was opposed to Newton's dualism of matter and spirit. Indeed Coleridge reserved the word "materialist" for those who believed in a matter different from spirit.

To this system Priestley added David Hartley's associationist (and necessarian) system of psychology to link necessarian causation with individual religious life. For Hartley the laws of psychological association built our sensations into complex ideas, and the development of these, when it worked as it should, led eventually to theopathy, the knowledge and love of God. Coleridge's psychological approach to religious states was the result of his adoption of Hartley, and, even after 1800, when he lost his trust in Locke and Hartley, he still, as we shall see, had a psychological approach to metaphysical questions.

It will be seen that the various parts of Priestley's system were bound together by the law of philosophical necessity, that is, of strict causation. It may be hard now to see the difference in result between this and the Tenth Article of the Thirty-nine, which also denies free will, but Coleridge thought necessarianism not only a corollary of Unitarianism but also a principle of the greatest moral importance. The main difference seems to be that where the Article asserts that we cannot do good by our free will without grace, the doctrine of necessity asserts that we have no independent power to do evil either. There may be sin but there can be no guilt, and this has important implications for how we, and God, ought to treat the sinner. We can see how it leads directly to Coleridge's Unitarian belief in the absolutely unlimited mercy of God.[14]

Though all this was based on an anti-Newtonian system, yet Newton himself had been a Unitarian. He was indeed an ambiguous figure with his own contribution still to make. In *Religious Musings* he appears among the Unitarian saints who rise to welcome the Second Coming at the first resurrection (the resurrection of the saints), and he is there described, in a figure apparently based on Hamlet's "one auspicious and one drooping eye," as "raising his serener eye to heaven."[15] The less serene eye is apparently that of the physicist and "materialist"; the more serene is that of the interpreter of biblical prophecy. Among his explanations of biblical prophecy Newton published a chapter on the meanings of the various symbols in the prophetic language which other interpreters could use, and which Priestley (and Coleridge) did use.

The Unitarians were strongly involved, even for nonconformists, in moves for religious toleration and political reform in England, and they welcomed, and were active in, the French Revolution, which many of them saw as the first stage of the apocalypse and the first step towards the millennium. When Priestley's radical sympathies led to the burning down of his house near Manchester by a king-and-country mob, and to his decision to migrate to the United States, he published two farewell sermons.[16] In these he likened the present state of Europe, and of the French Revolution, to the point in Revelation where the angel opens the fifth seal. Priestley's biblical faith meant that he looked forward to an actual resurrection of the dead, but he interpreted the prophecies of events of the last days preceding that as foretelling political events, for example, the fall of the stars as the fall of the great. He gave as his authority for these interpretations Newton's chapter on the prophetic language. We know that Coleridge knew of the sermons from his reference in *Religious Musings* to Priestley musing "expectant on these promised years," that is, the millennium; and we know that he noticed the reference to Newton because his early notebook contains a quotation (not the one used by Priestley) to that very chapter.[17] All this comparison with the last days did not (nor was it meant to) discourage the Unitarian fervor for, and involvement with, the French Revolution, or their expectation of the millennium, which Priestley interpreted as "the universal fraternity of love" and which Coleridge called "the vast family of Love."[18] Coleridge's pantisocracy, in which all men were to be brothers,[19] would have been a new-world variety of this.

Obviously it is easy enough to disagree with this, and indeed the Unitarian Church itself changed greatly in the course of the nineteenth century, but it is hard to see why some literary historians feel so much distaste for it. It is not at all uncommon to see it assumed that in the 1790s Coleridge was trying to escape from Unitarianism, that his reading was leading him away from it, that he was always orthodox at heart, or that he was already anticipating later ideas which were hostile to his then faith. These remarks usually carry some implied approval of the change, as if his conversion to orthodox Calvinism were, to scholars as scholars, necessarily a good thing.

Obvious support for the contemptuous opinions of Coleridge's earlier religious beliefs can be found in the many remarks which Coleridge the Trinitarian made when he was trying to distance himself from Coleridge the Unitarian. As late as the end of 1803, Coleridge still regarded the Unitarian doctrine that God was utterly impersonal (rather than consisting of three persons) as "the pure Fountain of all my moral and religious feelings,"[20] and he then still stigmatized the Trinitarians as "idolators" (his favorite phrase for them).[21] There was no sign of any change in opinion in 1804, but he was converted to a belief in the Trinity in a sudden rush "at 1.30 p.m. on 12 February, 1805." The conversion was quite complete, for at that very hour Coleridge went on to write a long note in which the Unitarian Priestley and the Arian Price were now themselves described as "idolators."[22] Thereafter all his references to his old faith in writing or in talk were hostile. It is all very human, but it is a pity that the *odium theologicum* has spilt over into some scholarly attitudes.

Coleridge's polemical spirit was not the only reason why critics have not looked to his religious views of the time for influence on his poetry. Another reason was his habit of insisting that any idea which he came to adopt was something that he had somehow anticipated intellectually or, at the very least, emotionally. This was an aspect of his character which De Quincey called "Coleridge's infirmity," which Lamb called "quizzing the world by lyes," and which made Hazlitt remark that "he never troubles himself about facts,"[23] though they all saw it as a weakness rather than a crime. The way it happened can be seen clearly in a note of 1805[24] that seems to mark his first reading of Schelling, in which he speaks of himself as seeking in objects of nature for a symbolic language for his own innate ideas which, even when it seems new, "is *Logos*, the Creator! and the Evolver!" The note goes on to ask, "What is the right, the virtuous Feeling, and consequent action, when a man having long meditated & perceived a certain Truth finds another, foreign writer, who has handled the same. . .? Joy!" The foreign writer who had handled these ideas must be Schelling and, as these ideas had never appeared before in Coleridge's writings, he must, in fact, be their source. Nevertheless this note, occurring as it does in a private notebook, is amiable self-deception, in which the wish was father to the thought, rather than deliberate imposture.

Nevertheless, many critics have been sufficiently imposed on to believe Coleridge's claims that he anticipated German idealist philosophy,[25] and quite a number of critics, trusting confidently to Coleridge's claims, have found that the Kantian or Schellingesque view of the mind is the informing spirit of Coleridge's poetry of 1795–98,[26] even though this means placing his shift away from Hartley up to a year before he christened his son Hartley[27] (indeed even before the latter's conception). In fact, there is no contemporaneous evidence for any of Coleridge's claims of "anticipation."[28] The position is much the same in regard to his religious opinions. Here Coleridge later claimed that he had always been a Trinitarian in philosophy, *ad normam Platonis*, that is to say, as a doctrine about the nature of man, though this Platonic doctrine only appeared in his writing on 12 February 1805, on the same page as the record of his religious conversion.[29] Similarly he claimed that he had always regarded Saint John as a Trinitarian, though on the only occasion on which he quoted a relevant passage from Saint John's Gospel in his early poetry he gave it a Unitarian explanation, and on the only occasion on which he used similar passages in prose it was as part of an *anti*-Trinitarian argument.[30] Again critics have accepted Coleridge's delusions and have taken the view that his early faith was something that he was seeking to escape from, and that the good things in his poetry only came about because he somehow anticipated the beliefs which he thought better in his later days. They are throwing away the substance of his faith for a shadow somehow cast backwards by the unimagined future.

Perhaps the most influential reason why many critics refuse to take Coleridge's professed faith of the 1790s seriously is the idea that it is not worth taking seriously—that by believing that God is the source of all action and by denying men free will, the faith abolished morality and obliterated any distinction between good and evil. This is a complete misunderstanding of the issues, for the paradox that a man is bound by moral laws even if he has no free will is no harder in necessarianism than in the Calvinist view of the doctrine of predestination set out in the Thirty-nine Articles. It is a paradox with which anyone wishing to reconcile scientific doctrine with morality must grapple, and, indeed, to a good many people the Unitarian position will seem to be the more morally acceptable, for it does not sentence the sinner by necessity to eternal damnation.

This last point, that Coleridge held to Unitarianism because he thought it morally superior to Trinitarianism, gets a backhanded illustration in his later defense of what he considered to be the implications of Trinitarianism. In his *Aids to Reflection*, published in 1826, he set out to defend:

Doctrines of Arbitrary Election and Reprobation, the Sentence to everlasting Torment by an eternal and necessitating Decree; vicarious Atonement, and the necessity of the Abasement, Agony and ignominious Death of a most Holy and meritorious Person, to appease the wrath of God.[31]

A modern reader might assume that this passage was ironical, but it was not: later in the book he castigated the Arminians, that element in the Church which believed in free will, for not believing in Calvinistic (that is to say, absolute) predestination and for doubting the doctrine of eternal damnation.[32] Nevertheless, in the passage just quoted the phrasing is so strong and makes the objections to his position so clear that he must have remembered what he himself once thought of such doctrines.

The Unitarian concept of God makes a belief in the atonement impossible, for, if Christ were only a man, he could not be thought of as offering an acceptable sacrifice to appease the wrath of God, and Coleridge's revulsion from the idea of the atonement as a sacrifice to appease God's wrath is well known. He called Anglican ministers "Moloch priests"[33] with a reference to the heathen god in the Old Testament who demanded the sacrifice of the firstborn; he explained to the congregation at Shrewsbury that he could not preach the Lord's Supper (which is supposed to commemorate the sacrifice) even if it cost him the appointment there;[34] and, even after he had become a Trinitarian, he did not take the sacrament again (after leaving Cambridge) until 1827,[35] a year after he had written *Aids to Reflection*. Indeed Wordsworth knew his dislike so well that he did not believe that Coleridge had ever again taken the sacrament, even after he had defended the doctrine.[36]

Thus for Coleridge Unitarianism offered a morally acceptable God and hence a foundation for his own moral beliefs, even if he later stigmatized this belief as pantheistic. Hegel distinguishes between amoral pantheism in which things are God (*Alles ist Gott*) and the moral Spinozan or oriental pantheism in which God is the essence of things[37] (or, to use a more modern phrase, the ground of being), and Coleridge made much the same point when discussing Spinoza in his *Biographia Literaria*.[38] Indeed he used this very distinction in a sometimes misunderstood letter of 20 March 1796, [39] in which he attacked Priestley, not for saying that God does everything, for he himself called God omnificent and was still in 1798 speaking of Priestley's "sublime theological works,"[40] but because Priestley had said that God *is* everything, and so, by implication, that things are God—the amoral pantheism, though Coleridge calls it atheism. For Coleridge in the 1790s God was "nature's Essence, Mind and Energy":[41] God as the essence and mind of nature was acceptable to the eighteenth-century view of the natural world, while the last epithet, "Energy," linked this God in nature with the God of religion. The God derived from Newtonian science had been an absentee God, a watchmaker who left the watch to run of itself; Coleridge's God was continually present and active in His world. It was an idea that received a number of successive enrichments from his reading of Priestley and Hartley, Cudworth, Berkeley, and Spinoza, who, from their different positions, all had something to contribute to this (though it should be noted that Cudworth was cited by Priestley in support of the latter's doctrine of God's action in Nature, so that he does not represent any great change[42]). What remained constant was Coleridge's belief in a natural world full of the divine energy and the divine presence.

This belief fitted very naturally with the eighteenth-century tradition of discovering God in nature, and with the idea that nature is the language of God, whether in the sense of the mid-eighteenth-century poets Akenside and Young, or in the sense of Berkeley. At the same time what Coleridge later called the pantheism of his early thought, that is to say, the extreme emphasis on God's immanence in nature rather than His transcendence of it, made that presence more intense and the poet's relationship with it more immediate.

This religious feeling for the experience of nature is a strong and obvious element in Coleridge's early poetry, but his Unitarian faith was also strongly biblical, and here he belonged to a tradition which took the biblical narrative both literally and allegorically. In its medieval form the tradition of biblical interpretation was fourfold, adding three kinds of symbolical interpretation to the literal meaning. By the eighteenth century the system had lost some of its authority, yet even at the end of that century biblical interpretation was still poised between the old literal and allegorical (or typological) interpretations and the new German historical-critical methods, which had then scarcely penetrated England.[43] The older ways were certainly far from dead: there was, for instance, a Methodist poem of the period which employed the allegorical method to combine a sea-voyage with the last judgment to produce a bizarre warning to the voyager through life.[44] Certainly Coleridge in 1795–96 gave a great deal of attention in his long poems to biblical prophecy and its interpretation, and the effect of this was to put him in possession of a very ancient symbolical system for spiritual matters and to help shape both his religious and his poetical feeling.

Thus at the beginning of his poetic career Coleridge was exploring two different kinds of symbolism—natural symbolism and the symbolism of biblical prophecy. They represent two fundamentally different types, the one being the actual and personal experience of God in his symbolism in nature, and the other a form of literary expression conveying firstly meaning but also emotion. The first kind of symbolism is found in those poems which record the poet's discovery of God in the experience of nature, and the culmination of this kind is to be found in the Conversation Poems published in *Lyrical Ballads*. But this produces a wider significance, for Coleridge's predecessors and successors as well as himself, in that any reference to the appearances of nature becomes a reference to the qualities of God. Thus the imagery of nature plays an important part in the major narrative and descriptive poetry that marks the *annus mirabilis*. In that year the biblical imagery is virtually concentrated in two poems, *The Ancient Mariner* and *Kubla Khan*. As with the natural imagery, there is a great development of power between 1795 and 1797, but here there is also a difference in the way the symbolism is used. Interpretations of biblical prophecy were sometimes literal and sometimes political, but the figurative language of the prophets was also a way of thinking about moral and spiritual experience. Thus, to take an obvious example, Hebrew thinking about hell begins with the figure of the burning rubbish heaps of Gehenna, as Hobbes pointed out,[45] and this was later reinforced in Revelation by the image of the burning asphalt on the surface of the salt and sterile Dead Sea, "the lake burning with fire and brimstone." Such images call attention to the metaphorical elements in the idea, and so stress the mental and spiritual states involved rather than ideas of actual place and physical torment. Coleridge was concerned with the whole prophetic story from the first paradise through the fall to the days of wrath and to paradise restored, and in the course of a couple of years his thinking ran the gamut from literal and political meaning to a point where his whole emphasis was on the spiritual and emotional. In short, he made the journey from the simplest form of biblical allegory to poetic symbolism.

To these two kinds of symbolism, which would have seemed to Coleridge to have been two forms of the divine word, must be added a third kind which is less fundamental, and that is the Gothic. There were two sources of Gothic imagery open to Coleridge, Percy's *Reliques* and the Gothic novels. These, and the exotic East, were an accepted eighteenth-century door into a world where marvel (and thence symbol) could work freely, and so it was for Coleridge. But the Gothic world, though it may sometimes act as no more than a strange setting, also often contains powerful daemonic and sometimes demonic forces, and such forces can pose important questions, particularly in a world where God expresses himself as energy. In 1796, in *Religious Musings* and *Ode to the Departing Year*, Coleridge described two fountains, one the divine fountain in heaven and the other the fountain of destruction in its volcanic cave.[46] But the purpose of this second fountain was to bring about the Last Days, and so it too was an expression of the divine will and it too was part of the divine unity.

The sense of divine unity was of central importance to Coleridge, and in the Conversation Poems the encounter with God in nature brings together all the multifarious activities of the world and reconciles his presence with energy and quiet, light and dark, and the secluded with the far-seen. Though darkness and energy are present, the diabolical or the sinister is not particularly the concern of the Conversation Poems, but, in the three long poems of the time, the darker and potentially evil side of things is pressing. In *Kubla Khan* and *The Ancient Mariner* it is resolved into millennial and paradisal bliss. In *Christabel*, where the biblical imagery of those poems disappears, we are left with a poem whose resolution, though hinted, was never fully worked out and which remains not an answer but a question.

2
Natural Symbolism and the Conversation Poems

COLERIDGE'S long inquiry for a religious faith that would satisfy him intellectually and morally began in Cambridge in 1794 and lasted all his life. There are two things to be kept in mind about this inquiry. In the first place Coleridge did not remain in any state of suspended judgment; he was always in possession of an active faith that he was anxious to preach. Secondly, it should not be thought of as a progress from un-satisfactory answers to a final solution. The later nineteenth-century belief that German idealist philosophy had discovered the truth of things no longer holds so firmly, and, in any case, Coleridge did not seem to reach any final resting place after he abandoned (if he did so) his last guide, Schelling. What matters is what he made of each stage in his thought, and it was his earlier ideas which underlay the literary achieve-ments that give him his general reputation.

In 1794, the last year which Coleridge spent at Cambridge, his tutor in mathematics was William Frend, the Unitarian who was brought before the Vice-Chancellor's court and expelled from his fellowship. Coleridge was one of his most enthusiastic supporters and quickly adopted his religious ideas. Early in 1795 the *Lectures on Revealed Religion*, which Coleridge gave at Bristol, showed that he had adopted all the main Unitarian positions and arguments. He had come to dislike intensely the doctrine of the atonement, a main target of Unitarian attack:[1] indeed he said towards the end of his life that this dislike had been the main reason for his rejection of the doctrine of the Trinity, with which it was associ-ated.[2] With this he rejected the companion doctrines of predestination and eternal damnation. His new faith in the benevolence of God meant that he also preached the Unitarian belief that, even for the wicked, the afterlife would begin with a period of re-education, after which they too would be admitted to eternal bliss.[3]

As we have seen, Coleridge's dislike of a wrathful God who demanded sacrifice remained with him all his life. There were other beliefs that lasted in the same way, even if the ways in which he stated them changed considerably. One of these was the belief that God was at once, and in the same way, the ground of physical being and of mental and moral being, a belief which he stated and restated in Priestleyan terms, Berkeleyan terms, Spinozan terms, and finally, following Schelling, in terms of the Logos. The Unitarian grounds for this belief were quasi-scientific, as befitted a system largely founded by the scientist Priestley, for he held what was to be known much later as the energy theory of matter. Hence, because they were both energy, matter and spirit were the same things under different names and were both manifestations of the Divine Spirit. While still at Cambridge, Coleridge drew from his college library the work of Boscovitch, which Priestley considered the main support for this theory.[4] (Presumably the book was recommended by Frend.) While he was first at Bristol he read Baxter on *The Immateriality of the Soul*,[5] another prop in Priestley's exposition of the doctrine. All this was, of course, quite different from the classic physics of Sir Isaac Newton, who sharply distinguished matter from mind—Coleridge throughout his life attacked all dualists, and particularly Newton, as what he called materialists. William Frend has been described as an anti-Newtonian[6] and it was possibly he who directed Coleridge's invective in this direction. The Unitarian doctrine had, as we shall see, implications for necessarianism and for God's judgment on men, but it also had important implications for Coleridge's attitude to nature as both the manifestation and the language of God, two ideas that remained prominent in his thought from this time on.

These metaphysical ideas were an important background in Coleridge's thought, but in his poetry it was his thinking about experience that counted. There were several strands to this, and one strand, which will be only mentioned now but dealt with more fully in a later chapter, was his thinking about the experiential meaning of biblical prophecy. Priestley, as might be expected in the period of the French Revolution, placed great stress on the literal fulfilment of the apocalyptic prophecies and the arrival of the millennium, but he also interpreted the millennium as the arrival of "the universal fraternity of love," a point which Coleridge, as we have seen earlier, took up in both his lectures and his poetry of 1795. From here his thinking about the apocalyptic story and paradise in terms of love and sterility, joy and despair, led him into the rich imagery of his greatest poetry. But for clarity this must be dealt with separately.

Meanwhile Coleridge's ideas on the relation of God to nature led him on to that particularly potent employment of natural imagery in his poetry that he shared with Wordsworth. At first, in 1795, he seemed to be going back rather than forward. In preparing for the *Lectures on Revealed Religion* he drew the poems of Akenside and Young from the Bristol Library and it was their ideas (and their phrases) that he reproduced in the lectures.

> The Omnipotent has unfolded to us the Volume of the World, that there we may read the Transcript of himself. In Earth or Air the meadow's purple stores, the Moons mild radiance, or the Virgins form Blooming with rosy smiles, we see portrayed the bright impressions of the eternal Mind.[7]

That is Akenside, word for word. Another passage seems to owe more to Young.

> To the philanthropic Physiognomist a Face is beautiful because its Features are the symbols and visible signs of the inward Benevolence or Wisdom—to the pious man all Nature is thus beautiful because its every Feature is the Symbol and all its Parts the written Language of infinite Goodness and allpowerful Intelligence.[8]

This is clearly related to a passage he wrote about the same time as part of his contribution to *Joan of Arc:*

> For all that meets the bodily sense I deem
> Symbolical, one mighty alphabet
> For infant minds.[9]

In the volume of Young which Coleridge had borrowed there is a passage describing the heavens as a "Golden Alphabet" by which man could learn to read God in nature. In both these passages Coleridge is using the word "symbol" in its sense of a single alphabetical letter to be used in reading God's "Transcript of himself," while in the prose passage there is some play on the word's more general meaning of sign. In *Religious Musings* he went on to an illustration based on the Unitarian explanation of such controversial texts as "He that hath seen me hath seen the Father," which Priestley explained as meaning that what was seen was behavior from which God's qualities could be inferred.[10] The resemblance of this to the doctrine of the *Lectures* can be seen.

> For chiefly in the oppressed Good Man's face
> The Great Invisible (by symbols seen)
> Shines with peculiar and concentred lilght,

> When all of Self regardless the scourg'd Saint
> Mourns for th'oppressor. . .
> Who thee beheld thy imag'd Father saw.[11]

In the 1797 edition of the poem this leads into Akenside's view of natural symbolism.

> Fair the vernal mead,
> Fair the high grove, the sea, the sun, the stars;
> True impress each of their creating sire![12]

Thus Coleridge early had a clear theory of natural symbolism and of the discovery of God in nature, but his ideas were not new and certainly not an anticipation of later philosophies. These ideas alone would not be enough to account for the greater depth of response to landscape, the greater attention to its detail, the greater significance, the desire "to achieve a unity with Nature which is almost visionary in mood" which critics have found in Coleridge when compared with his predecessors.[13] To understand this we must digress into the part played by Hartley's system of psychology in Coleridge's religion. Hartley's psychology had been adopted by Priestley and his followers as part of Unitarianism and it was a logically necessary part of the system, making the necessitarian link between God's action and man's religious life. God's presence in all parts of his creation provided its ultimate unity, so that all apparent evil must be ultimate good and all apparent disharmony ultimate harmony. Through Hartley's psychology this applied also to the world of man. If God acted on man through sense-impressions, and if the landscape was, in effect, his language, then all his diverse effects in human beings must ultimately be a harmony. In what was Coleridge's first really successful poem he set out to grapple with this problem of reconciling God's unity with the world's diversity and produced the first of the Conversation Poems, "The Eolian Harp." The problem was one which long interested him and as late as 1799, in describing the attitude of Spinoza, the philosopher who then engaged him, he wrote:

> I would make a pilgrimage to the burning sands of Arabia or &c &c to find the Man who could explain to me there can be *oneness*, there being infinite Perceptions—yet there must be a *oneness*, not an intense Union but an absolute Unity.[14]

W. J. Bate rightly connected this note with the theme of "The Eolian Harp."[15] The Unitarian background to Coleridge's special concern for this unity can be seen in *Religious Musings:*

> 'Tis the sublime of man,
> Our noontide Majecty, to know ourselves
> Parts and proportions of one wondrous whole!
> This fraternises man, this constitutes
> Our charities and bearings. But 'tis God
> Diffused through all, that doth make all one whole.[16]

The passage leads on to make this understanding the basis for that universal sympathy and love which is the millennial paradise. It is a point which was to be important in *The Ancient Mariner.*

At the end of 1795 Coleridge had to hand an "Effusion" which he had begun a little earlier. It was quite short, using an image which he had used several times before, that of the Eolian harp played on by the breeze. In this case, in a figure addressed to Sara, the caresses of the wind bring from the lute, as the lover will from the coy maid, sweet upbraidings and then delicious surges of music. To this Coleridge added two further sections. In the first he began by comparing the aimless thoughts and fantasies flitting through his mind with the sound produced in the lute by the random breeze and went on, in an image based on the relation between the single instrument and the orchestra, to speculate that all of animated nature may be such harps, acted on by God to produce their individual tunes and hence his universal harmony: what might seem aimless in the single life is an harmonious part of the whole.

> And what if all of animated Life
> Be but as instruments diversely fram'd
> That tremble into thought, while thro' them breathes
> One infinite and intellectual breeze,
> And all in different heights so aptly hung,
> That murmurs indistinct and Bursts sublime,
> Shrill Discords and most soothing Melodies,
> Harmonious from Creation's vast concent—.
> Thus *God* would be the universal Soul,
> Mechaniz'd matter as the organic harps
> And each one's Tunes be that which each calls I.[17]

This he finally condensed into a form that stressed the direct action of God on men's minds as well as his all-consciousness and his all-inclusiveness:

> And what if all of animated nature
> Be but organic Harps diversely fram'd,

> That tremble into thought, as o'er them sweeps
> Plastic and vast, one intellectual breeze,
> At once the Soul of each, and God of all![18]

This is a necessarian and pantheistic metaphor[19]—pantheistic because God is "the Soul of each" and necessarian because the sound (the metaphorical equivalent of thought) is produced by the direct action of the breeze which is God. (A moment's reflection will make it obvious that the strings sound because they are acted upon while to tremble is, by dictionary definition, an involuntary act: attempts to read this as an anti-Hartleyan poem[20] ignore both language and logic.) Coleridge later confirmed the meaning of the figure when he quoted the poem in his *Philosophical Lectures* of 1819 to illustrate a pantheism of which he then disapproved,[21] and when he used the image of the breeze and the harp in *Biographia Literaria* to illustrate the Hartleyan system of psychology.[22]

This passage is followed by a palinode, felt by many critics to be rather odd, in which he submits to the rebuke of Sara for his indulgence in vain philosophy. What Sara here particularly points out is that he has forgotten that God is incomprehensible, and that the proper response to him is simply awe and deep feeling. What makes this conclusion odd is the suggestion that Coleridge could indeed have been satisfied with such a fideistic, know-nothing response to God. Certainly he let the speculations stand as, apparently, the main purpose of the poem. Both in the rather vapid effusion to Sara that begins the poem and in the speculations that follow, Coleridge is concerned with response, harmony, and unity, first between the lover and the beloved, and then between God and man. Nevertheless the poem as a whole is very poorly unified and the warmth given by the figure of the lover, and perhaps by the implied parallel of God with the lover, is thoroughly dissipated by the frigid and pietistic conclusion.

The next of the Conversation Poems, "Reflections on having left a place of retirement," also began from a Hartleyan idea, though this connection is not immediately obvious, and it issued in something vital to his future development. Like its predecessor the poem was set at Clevedon and dated 1795, but it was probably written a good many months after he had left the cottage there. It first appeared in print in *The Monthly Magazine* of October 1796, and if he had had the poem available in any form when his *Poems* were being printed in March 1796, then it seems most improbable that he would have withheld it. The poem is constructed on the same pattern of sections dealing with domestic bliss, relationship with God, and pious duty, as "The Eolian Harp" and, as in that poem, the only part that rises above mediocrity is the middle section, here describing an encounter with the nature of God on the summit of the stony mount that lies between Clevedon and the sea.

> Oh! what a goodly scene! *Here* the bleak mount,
> The bare bleak mountain speckled thin with sheep;
> Grey clouds, that shadowing spot the sunny fields;
> And river, now with bushy rocks o'er-brow'd,
> Now winding bright and full, with naked banks;
> And seats, and lawns, the Abbey and the wood,
> And cots, and hamlets, and faint city-spire;
> The channel *there*, the Islands and white sails,
> Dim coasts, and cloud-like hills, and shoreless ocean—[23]

It is a comment on the making of a poem, and on its relation to the experience it claims to describe, that this seems to owe something to an earlier poem describing a view seen "while climbing the left ascent of Brockley Coomb" in May, 1795.

> Ah! what a luxury of landscape meets
> My gaze! Proud towers, and Cots more dear to me,
> Elm-shadow'd Fields, and prospect-bounding Sea!
> Deep sighs my lonely heart: I drop the tear:
> Enchanting spot! O were my Sara here![24]

What, then, accounts for the difference in the depth of the description, and then for what follows in the later poem—a description of the ecstasy of knowing God in the landscape?

> It seemed like Omnipresence! God, methought,
> Had built him there a Temple: the whole World
> Seem'd *imag'd* in its vast circumference:
> No *wish* profan'd my overwhelmed heart.
> Blest hour! It was a luxury,—to be![25]

Coleridge had described such an ecstasy, rather more didactically and less as experience, earlier in 1796 in his *Religious Musings*. What made Hartley's psychology particularly attractive to Unitarians was his belief that the sense-impressions which built up complex ideas came from God and that they could lead eventually to theopathy, or the knowledge and love of God. Coleridge described this culmination:

> Strong to believe whate'er of mystic good
> The Eternal dooms for His immortal sons.
> From Hope and firmer Faith to perfect Love

> Attracted and absorbed: and centered there
> God only to behold, and know, and feel,
> Till by exclusive consciousness of God
> All self-annihilated it shall make
> God its Identity: God all in all!
> We and our Father one![26]

To this Coleridge added triumphantly:

> See this *demonstrated* by Hartley. . . . See it likewise proved, and freed
> from the charge of Mysticism, by Pistorius in his Notes and Additions.

Theopathy of this sort may not be technically mystical but this nature-ecstasy is at the heart of what is new in the nature poetry of Coleridge and Wordsworth. Here Coleridge drew for the first time in an actual landscape on his theory that the character of God can be read in the features of a scene, and at the same time he made the encounter with a particular landscape an encounter with God. Of course, in traditional mysticism the encounter with God is not normally mediated by a landscape, but in this case landscape was the way in which Coleridge brought his longing for union to a focus and to an ecstasy, which there is no reason to think feigned. Certainly in the Conversation Poems of 1797 and 1798 the search for God in nature continued to be just such a search for union and ecstasy, and, whether or not it was a change in his theory of natural symbolism, it was a change in his experience of it.

From the time that Coleridge and Wordsworth became close friends in June 1797, Coleridge's letters show that they were engaged in close discussions of nature and poetry. Wordsworth's ideas were not radically different from Coleridge's, for these ideas were rooted in late eighteenth-century thought, and those who wish to make one or the other poet the sole source only show that, between them, both had something to contribute. Perhaps Wordsworth's ideas were less thoroughly worked out, were less involved with formal philosophy or religion, and appeared less frequently in his writings (though appear they did). Nevertheless, there is one point that shows Wordsworth's independence of Coleridge, and this concerns their experience of ecstasy. Coleridge's experience was based on the idea that God could be "read" in nature, reinforced now by the Berkeleyan idea that nature is the language of God (for he had declared himself a Berkeleyan in the previous December), and it also depended on the old, widely known idea that the beauty of the world provides an intuition of God. But it is not mystical in the strict sense of the word, that is to say, it was not the same experience as that of the great mystics. It is true that towards the end of 1796, in the revisions of *Joan of Arc,* which he then called "The Visions of the Maid of Orleans," he described a state of trance, into which Joan is thrown by her discovery of the wickedness and misery about her and in which she becomes aware of a "Presence" who, as "A horror of great darkness wrapt her round," calmed her soul;[27] but this, though it may hint at the moral illumination which the mystical experience brings, is still not strictly a mystical experience. (The "horror of great darkness" is a biblical quotation,[28] not a personal experience.). Certainly this revision was to have been, and perhaps was, sent to Wordsworth at the end of 1796, and his attention would have been further drawn to it when the "Visions" were published in the *Morning Post* of 26 December 1797, [29] and perhaps that "Presence" had a reverberation in *Tintern Abbey.* But, all the same, Wordsworth's experiences went back to his boyhood,[30] and nothing in Coleridge's writing suggests that he would have been able to communicate to Wordsworth those marks which show the latter's mature experiences to be authentic. Unlike Coleridge's tentative and never wholly fulfilled explorations, Wordsworth's experience was the same as that described by the mystics, Western or Eastern, and this is all the more remarkable because he seems to have had no knowledge of the tradition. Like them he described the darkness in which the light of sense failed or slept, the encounter with the presence behind appearances, and the moral illumination and certainty that followed, even if that could not be translated into ordinary language. But though Coleridge's experiences could not claim the weight of this tradition, they were nevertheless intuitions of God in the world and, as Coleridge insisted in poems and letters, they had moral consequences for ordinary life. Certainly we see Coleridge from the beginning of the friendship exploring the meaning of the experience.

The word which the two poets chose to express this intuition of God and of moral meaning in the forms of nature was imagination. Wordsworth worked the word into a revised poem in which he spoke of the forms of nature as "the holy forms /Of young imagination."[31] Wherever the word came from Coleridge worked out the idea further in one of his letters, which, Gabriel Marcel remarks, shows the nature of his pantheism and how it attaches to his then theory of the imagination.[32] He had earlier, in a different context, quoted a passage of Madame Roland's which claimed that the atheist seems to lack a sense compared to the religious man and to seek a syllogism where the believer finds an action of grace.[33] Coleridge found the distinction illuminating and on 16 October 1797, he wrote, after discussing the importance of children's tales:

I know no other way of giving the mind a love of 'the Great' & 'the Whole'.—Those who have been led to the same truths step by step thro' the constant testimony of their senses, seem to me to want a sense which I possess. . . . They . . . uniformly put the negation of a power for the possession of a power—& called the want of imagination Judgement.

In another letter of 14 October he wrote:

It is only in the faith of something *great*—something *one* and *indivisible* that rocks or waterfalls, mountains or caverns give me the sense of sublimity or majesty! But in this faith *all things* counterfeit infinity.

The curious phrase "counterfeit infinity" has been traced[34] to the seventeenth-century Platonist Ralph Cudworth, who used it in explaining that God is the only true infinity. Mathematical infinities, whether in number, size, or duration, can always be added to, and so, far from being true infinities, they can only counterfeit or imitate infinity. What presumably attracted Coleridge was the idea that a physical object could imitate infinity, and this would be no disadvantage in the language of God. When one puts this idea of the imagination that can sense the great and indivisible—that is, God—in nature together with the idea that the appearances of nature are the language of God, one can then understand the faith and intensity with which Coleridge set out to read and understand that language.

The poem of his own that Coleridge quoted to illustrate the second of these letters was "This Lime-tree Bower My Prison," written in the June of 1797. This follows the typical pattern of the Conversation Poems, beginning in domestic seclusion (if only for a few lines), rising to a wider contact with God in nature, and returning to draw the moral meaning from this. What is noticeable here is that in all the sections of the poem there is a vivid and loving detail in the natural descriptions, more intense here than in any of the earlier poems.

> The roaring dell, o'erwooded, narrow, deep,
> And only speckled by the mid-day sun;
> Where its slim trunk the ash from rock to rock
> Flings arching like a bridge;—that branchless ash,
> Unsunn'd and damp, whose few poor yellow leaves
> Ne'er tremble in the gale, yet tremble still,
> Fann'd by the waterfall! and there my friends
> Behold the dark green file of long lank weeds,
> That all at once (a most fantastic sight!)
> Still nod and drip beneath the dripping edge
> Of the blue clay-stone.[35]

Though the description is of water and plants, yet the active verbs—*roar, fling, tremble, fan, nod*—suggest a powerful life that makes the scene a suggestion of the power and activity of God in nature.

This scene makes a poetical preparation for the central passages of the poem, in which God actively reveals himself in the landscape. Coleridge tampered with the passage in his old age, but the earliest version, given in a letter to Southey of 17 July 1797, reads:

> So my friend
> Struck with joy's deepest calm, and gazing round
> On the wide view, may gaze till all doth seem
> Less gross than bodily; a living Thing
> That acts upon the mind, and with such hues
> As cloathe the Almighty Spirit, when he makes
> Spirits perceive his presence!

Coleridge attached to the word "view" a note which read, "You remember I am a *Berkleian*," so that the communication between God and man through the hues of the landscape is deliberate, part of the language of God. There have been discussions as to whether the phrase "less gross than bodily" can apply to God, and as to whether the spirits who perceive his presence can be men. In the previous year Coleridge had said that, because he was a Berkeleyan, he did not believe in an incarcerated soul or spirit in man: by implication he believed that man was spirit, physically and mentally—"I am a mere *apparition*—a naked Spirit," he wrote to Thelwall on 31 December 1796. A further corollary is that God, the essence of nature, is perceived in the landscape which is his language and so he cannot be wholly different from the bodily landscape any more than man, as Coleridge then saw him, could be different from spirit. There is a unity of *kind* between man, landscape, and God that brings out the deeper religious quality which Coleridge now found in the perception of nature.

When Coleridge returned his thought to the bower in which he sat, his conclusion was that nature will employ even its more humble and ordinary aspects to keep the heart "awake to love and beauty." This is an implication of the vision at the center of the poem, and it embodies a feeling about such experiences that is older than Coleridge's particular theories about them: it is one whole side of the religious debate about man's nature and his relation to his world. What the poem, and other romantic poems like it, do is to take the sense of man's natural kinship with the divine, and the sense of the goodness and health of his natural and ordinary emotions, and attach them to aspects of experience that are most felt as enduring, beautiful, and symbolic—symbolic because they represent to us those intuitions about the goodness of God, of natural man, and of the natural world—beautiful because of the sanction and reassurance they give. In this way the poem is part of a long tradition of contemplating and describing nature, but this does not diminish its own importance or its originality. It makes man part of nature as well as making nature divine, and it places both in an intimate relation with God. It was this seamless relationship which justified the natural feelings that were so powerfully attractive to the romantics, as well as inspiring those feelings in the first place, but it is important to realize that for Coleridge this was not a well-worn commonplace but something that came to him through his own religious beliefs and insights.

The letters of October bring us down to the period when *Kubla Khan* and *The Ancient Mariner* were writtten. The next of the Conversation Poems, "Frost at Midnight," came in February 1798, when Coleridge was writing in a letter that he had finished *The Ancient Mariner* and when he was also writing to Thomas Poole a long description of his life as an often homesick schoolboy at Christ's Hospital. This homesickness was certainly something less terrible than the loneliness of the Mariner, but the Conversation Poems are personal where the long poems are universal. Here, the poem begins with darkness and solitude, the solitude of the poet writing alone at midnight, looking for companionable life and finding it only in the flapping of the film on the grate. From here it moves back in time to the schoolboy watching the same thing and longing for some contact with his family. The resolution this time does not lie in a personal encounter with God, but in a magnificent passage which might be described as yet another gloss, and a more contemporary one, on *The Ancient Mariner,* describing the presence of God everywhere in nature and the whole of nature as his language.

> But *thou,* my babe! shalt wander like a breeze
> By lakes and sandy shores, beneath the crags
> Of ancient mountain, and beneath the clouds,
> Which image in their bulk both lakes and shores
> And mountain crags: so shalt thou see and hear
> The lovely shapes and sounds intelligible
> Of that eternal language, which thy God
> Utters, who from eternity doth teach
> Himself in all, and all things in himself.[36]

From here the poem returns to the cycle of the seasons, and finally to the frost, as part of the secret ministry of nature.

If "Frost at Midnight" forms a kind of personal subscript to *The Ancient Mariner,* the last of the Conversation Poems of the year bears a similar relation to *Christabel.* It was finished in early May 1798,[37] and, while the first writing of *Christabel* cannot be dated exactly, that must also have been at about this time. Certainly there is one very obvious link. The first part of *Christabel* (the part written in this year) ends with a "Conclusion" in which a chorus of nightbirds, in this case owls, celebrate the couching together of Christabel and Geraldine. There is something at least sinister about their rejoicing, but it is followed by Christabel's visionary dream, in which joy seems to swallow up distress. In the uncompleted long poem this vision was never fully worked out, nor the daemonic fully taken up and resolved, but when we turn to the Conversation Poem, there is no doubt about the joy. Here the nightbirds are not owls but nightingales, full of daemonic energy[38] and also full of joy. In the first part of the poem Coleridge insists that the tradition of the melancholy nightingale is false, these are the birds of joy. And the main part of the poem is the realization of this as the birds crowd singing through the whole wood:

> till the moon
> Emerging, hath awakened earth and sky
> With one sensation, and those wakeful birds
> Have all burst forth in choral minstrelsy,
> As if some sudden gale had swept at once
> A hundred airy harps! And she hath watched
> Many a nightingale perch giddily
> On blossomy twig still swinging from the breeze,
> And to that motion tune his wanton song
> Like tipsy Joy that reels with tossing head.[39]

This is a Dionysian rout, even to the tossing of the head.[40] The poem is full of extraordinary elation, life, and vigor. In *Christabel* the darknesss had been a threatening, alien territory, but in this poem the wish for young Hartley, "that with the dark he may associate joy," has been fully acted out, and the whole poem shows that Coleridge had captured the world of the darkness and the daemonic for joy.

The Conversation Poems of Coleridge's great year have here been treated in their conjunction with the very different long poems because only in that way can they be given their full weight. The Conversation Poems record Coleridge's search for encounter with God, and, naturally, what they record is the joy of discovery. There is no place in them for the darker parts of life. When we turn to Keats's "Ode to a Nightingale" we find what is missing in Coleridge's poem:

> The weariness, the fever, and the fret,
> Here where men sit and hear each other groan.[41]

It is the same when we compare the Conversation Poems as a whole, "Wordsworthian" though they sound and great as they are as expressions of the "Wordsworthian" joy, with Wordsworth's own lyric poetry. Wordsworth used his feeling for Nature and the natural order to face and comprehend deep and disturbing emotions, to explore dark passages. His faith is based on the experience and the conquest of suffering and misery. As against this, when Coleridge wrote:

> A melancholy bird? Oh! idle thought!
> In Nature there is nothing melancholy[42]

he was expressing triumphantly a moment of almost mystical exultation. For that moment of insight to be valid, there had to be somewhere else in his thought a facing of the deep problems involved. For insight into the more intense and disturbing parts of his being, and for his attempts to find joy even through them, we must turn to the sometimes very different symbols of the great poems, which provide at once a mask and a revelation. In these poems Coleridge was freed to express such feelings by his use of vision, reverie, and Gothic narrative, but the license and the distancing which these forms gave him would not have been enough in themselves. What enabled him to explore and express this world of feelings was the new symbolic mode which he developed.

3
Biblical, Natural, and Gothic Symbolism in
The Ancient Mariner

EARLY in 1795, when Coleridge was first developing his theories of natural symbolism, he also became interested in a form of literary symbolism, though he did not then apply that word to it. This was biblical symbolism or "the prophetic language," a description of which he found in Sir Isaac Newton's works of Prophecy. It was a method that belonged to the past, allegorical and, in its way, straightforward. It found what were sometimes moral applications, but more usually political, historical, and future-historical senses in the books of the Old Testament prophets and in Saint John's Revelation. It was in this straightforward way that Coleridge first employed the "language," using its figures of speech in his early poems and constructing new (and sometimes absurd) figures on the same lines. However, by 1797 the apocalyptic story had come to express some of Coleridge's inner feelings, particularly his obsessive guilt and his hope of joy, and it was as symbolism of feeling that this language entered into *Kubla Khan* and *The Ancient Mariner*. It is, of course, not the only kind of symbolism in *The Ancient Mariner* for there is, along with the apocalyptic symbolism, also both Gothic symbolism and symbolism of nature. The function of the Gothic mode would seem to be to provide a setting and (because realism was not expected in a Gothic tale) a poetic credibility for the other two sets of symbols which, closely intermingled, dominate the core of the poem, reinforcing each other, though each carried its own system of implications. What the biblical symbols brought with them was the outline of the apocalyptic story in which they were originally embedded.

The importance of the apocalyptic theme in English romantic poetry has been pointed out more than once, as has been its adaptation from a religious or political scheme to a pattern for individual development.[1] In the early 1790s, in nonconformist radical circles stimulated by the French

Revolution (and not only among Unitarians), it was widely taken as a prophecy of events that would happen in the very near future, to be interpreted initially as an allegory of political revolution, but often as moving on to a literal forecast of natural and supernatural events. Sermons on the subject were common: at Cambridge Frend's supporter, Edward Garnham, preached on the subject in Trinity College chapel in December 1793, while in 1796 *The British Critic* had the task of reviewing, belatedly, a sermon which had calculated a general resurrection of the dead "in late 1795 or thereabouts." (The reviewer treated it quite seriously.) Coleridge's own acquaintance with the theme came from two sermons by Joseph Priestley which, besides giving him the subject for his poem *Religious Musings,* introduced him to Sir Isaac Newton's interpretation of the language of biblical prophecy.[2]

The meanings which Newton assigned to the various prophetic symbols were usually political or historical. Among the interpretations which Coleridge used in his early polemical poems were earthquakes as wars, the fall of the stars from heaven as the political fall of the great, fog obscuring the sun as attempts to suppress, in this case, the Revolution, and whoredom as apostasy, here the whoredom of the Established Church with the Daemon Power.[3] In applying the prophecies to the current situation, Coleridge sometimes attempted to elaborate the figures in what turned out to be a thoroughly pedestrian and ludicrous way. The baleful magnificence of Saint John's imagination was not improved when his locusts—creatures with crowns of gold, faces like men, scales like breastplates of iron, and tails like scorpions—were translated with careful attention to the allegory:

> Shrieked AMBITION'S ghastly throng
> And with them those the locust Fiends that crawl'd
> And glittered in Corruption's slimy track.[4]

Those shrieking locusts amused even Coleridge himself later on, but they were not the only examples of this kind of writing. Taking Newton's interpretation of riding in clouds as ruling and of the movement of clouds as wars, Coleridge had Envy in a French cloud and Oppression in an English one pursue each other over Europe to represent the Revolutionary wars, while the interpretation of the birth of a child as the establishment of a new kingdom produced the figure of the birth of twins to symbolize nature's struggle to bring forth equality and peace.[5] As a set of symbols they were a very rum lot, connected only by the apocalyptic prophecies and hence, for Coleridge at this time, by his interpretation of current events. But this was not the only possible interpretation of the apocalyptic story.

The apocalypse has always been the subject of disputed interpretations. The idea goes back to the prophecies of Isaiah and Ezekiel in the days of the Babylonian exile of the Hebrews. One part of these prophecies, that concerning the Messiah, was fulfilled for Christians by the life of Christ; another part, relating to the day of wrath, the restoration of Jerusalem, and the establishment of God'd kingdom on earth, remained to be accomplished at the second coming of Christ in his glory. In the Christian scheme, as Saint Paul explained,[6] there are to be two stages, the first when Christ returns and raises his own from the dead, and the second when he delivers the kingdom to God the Father, when there will be a general resurrection. In the first century, when these things were daily expected, Saint John at Patmos wrote his Revelation, a series of visions elaborating the symbolism and the prophetic scheme of the Old Testament prophets and interpreting them in a Christian context to foretell the terrors of the day of wrath, the first resurrection of the saints, the millennium or thousand-year rule of the saints under Christ, then the general resurrection and judgment, and finally the descent of the New Jerusalem. In later years the obscure visions which made up the earlier part of this book sometimes embarrassed Christian teachers and apologists. It was not until the fourth century that the book's position in the canon was secure, and even before that Origen had written an explanation of it as simply an allegory of the individual spiritual life and not a prophecy of temporal events. Since then interpretations have run the gamut from literal prophecy to spiritual allegory.

Coleridge wavered between treating the prophecies as political allegory, spiritual allegory, and factual truth. Of course one can never be absolutely sure that his poetical beliefs coincided with his prose ones, and he might have regarded the matter as merely a suitably Miltonic theme for his poetical ambitions, but that would not mean that he did not take it very seriously. He immersed himself in the subject, calling his periodical *The Watchman* after Ezekiel, the Watchman of Israel, and making frequent references to Revelation in his footnotes. His imagination was also captured by Burnet's *The Sacred Theory of the Earth*, a "scientific" demonstration that natural forces could and would produce the pestilences and plagues of the last days and the restoration of paradise. He formed a project for a poem based on part of that book[7] and he looked elsewhere, particularly in the poems of Erasmus Darwin, the scientist and poet, for more up-to-date "scientific" explanations of the days of wrath and of the paradisal climate of the millennium.[8] Though some of the apocalyptic description in the poems of 1795–96 can be explained as political allegory of the Revolution, there are passages, for instance those dealing with the fiery whirlwinds and based on Burnet and Darwin, which seem quite literal, and certainly the descriptions of the millennium and the resurrection cannot be taken in any other way.

Though the main theme of *Religious Musings* was an account of the coming apocalypse, both political and supernatural, Coleridge also used certain incidents in his story as sources of spiritual allegory. There is no evidence that the young Coleridge was familiar with Origen or with the tradition of spiritual interpretation, but it was natural for him to think of allegorizing the inner life. Though his religion was necessarian, without belief in free will, yet its roots in Hartleyan psychology meant that it was introspective and concerned with the history of moral feelings. His first attempt at such allegorizing was explained by him thus (with a curiously exact image of sublimation):

> Our evil Passions, under the influence of Religion, become innocent, and may be made to animate our virtue—in the same manner as the thick mist melted by the Sun, increases the light which it had before excluded. In the preceding paragraph, agreeably to this truth, we had allegorically narrated the transfiguration of Fear into holy Awe.[9]

The preceding paragraph he mentions describes a "trembling wretch" pursued by "Hunter-fiends" finding refuge in an altar in the wilderness and thence seeing that the vials of wrath are in truth filled with "renovating love." The doctrine that God's wrath and his love are the same is not an easy one, even in Unitarianism, and Coleridge's lines add very little. The best that can be said for the passage is that, as an image of flight and terror, it does perhaps represent in its own turgid way the experience of the poet who ran away from home as a child, and from Cambridge as a young man, and who was later to write:

> Like one that on a lonesome road
>   Doth walk in fear and dread,
> And having once turned round walks on,
>   And turns no more his head;
> Because he knows a frightful fiend
>   Doth close behind him tread.[10]

The passage in *Religious Musings* was unpromising either as allegory or as poetry, but a later and better passage in the same poem used the vision of paradise as a simile for the silent spirit's foretaste of bliss, and, in likening this delight to "fragments wild . . . of unearthly melodies" that float from heaven to earth, the simile is close to symbol.[11]

 In this poem the literal and the allegorical interpretations of the apocalypse seem to coexist, as well they might in such instances as the one just mentioned. There was at least on point in the Unitarian treatment of the story that might lead Coleridge to spiritual allegory, and this was Priestley's idea that the millennium was "the universal fraternity of love," an idea which Coleridge adopted both in the *Lectures on Revealed Religion* and in *Religious Musings:*

> he by sacred sympathy might make
> The whole one Self! Self, that no alien knows!
> Self, far diffused as Fancy's wing can travel!
> Self, spreading still! Oblivious of its own,
> Yet all of all possessing! This is Faith!
> This the Messiah's destined victory![12]

On the other hand the apocalypse story is full of horrors and of the pouring out of the vials of wrath, and, even for those Unitarians (among them Coleridge) who believed that God's terrors were educative in purpose, the terror remained. Thus the apocalypse story provided a paradigm of terror, torment, and isolation ("a sordid solitary thing") resolved in the salvation of becoming part of "the vast family of Love."

Coleridge, of course, did not believe in guilt: as there was no free will there could be no condemnation, only "the final happiness of all men," and hell would be a temporary state in which "the wicked will during [this] period be suffering the remedies adapted to their several bad habits."[13] As he wrote to Thelwall on 13 May 1796,

> We mean these men when we say—Men of bad *principles. Guilt* is out of the Question—I am a Necessarian, and of course deny the possibility of it.

He was of the same opinion in 1798.[14] Nevertheless, it is one thing not to believe in the possibility of guilt and quite another not to feel it, and Coleridge seems to have suffered from what can only be called neurotic guilt for most of his life (the patterns of such feeling are set early in life and in Coleridge's case there are signs in his childhood). "The Pains of Sleep" with its glimpses of "the unfathomable hell within," in which "all seemed guilt, remorse and woe," belonged to a later year, 1803, and may owe something to opium; but a fragment of the same date[15] tells us that such dreams had "been often so," and his early history was as full of flights and regrets as his later, while in "The Pains of Sleep," the remedy, "To be beloved is all I need," is no different from that in *Religious Musings*. This does not mean that Coleridge's interest was psychiatric; his thought and feelings were inescapably religious and the apocalyptic story, even on a Unitarian reading, is the story of how God frees the soul from the pains of sin and death and raises it in the bliss of paradise. What it does mean is that Coleridge was peculiarly fitted to explore this story: we must realize that Coleridge's concern with paradise was much more than a literary or antiquarian interest; it was a state to which he desperately aspired.

There is an interesting notebook entry of late 1796 whose purpose is uncertain. It consists of loose quotations, apparently from memory, drawn from various places in Boehme's *Aurora*,[16] their common thread being their connection with the apocalypse; they are followed by a passage when, as John Beer remarks, Coleridge goes off on his own speculations, and this part is a free meditation on damnation, desolation, and terror:

> Why sleep ye, O ye Watchman—
> Wake from the sleep of whoredom. trim your Lamp—
> Sound, sound the Trumpets—for the Bridegroom comes—
> O man, thou half-dead Angel—
> a dusky light—a purple *flash*
> crystalline splendor—light blue—
>   *Green* lightnings.—
> in that eternal & delirious misery—
>   wrathfires—
>   inward desolations
>   an horror of great darkness
>   great things that on the ocean
>   counterfeit infinity—[17]

Given Coleridge's disbelief in eternal damnation, these can hardly be notes for a sermon. What they do look like are the groups of phrases for use in poems that one often finds in this notebook. Certainly they combine the vivid colors, the ocean, and the deathfires of *The Ancient Mariner* with the terror and desolation of the days of wrath in the apocalypse. At least that part of the story had by this date entered Coleridge's imagination as the embodiment of guilt and misery. What needed to be added to it was the healing escape to love and paradise.

The appearance of the ocean in this imagery is a reminder that Coleridge was also developing his ideas on natural symbolism and that the ocean had already appeared in his poetry, but associated with the infinite in a context of ecstasy (just as later, in a letter, the curious phrase "counterfeit infinity" was also to recur in a context of ecstasy):

> Dim coasts, and cloud-like hills, and shoreless Ocean—
> It seem'd like Omnipresence![18]

The Mariner was to find on his ocean the sense of infinity both as omnipresence and beauty and as isolation and horror; for the apocalypse story was a redemption story containing heaven as well as hell, and it was to appear much more fully in the poem than it did in the note. Nevertheless, the ocean can be seen as a natural symbol, and natural and biblical symbols blend inextricably in the Mariner's story.

Not only the sea itself but the sea voyage had symbolical associations. If we examine the voyage in the poem we find connections that both lead forward and point backward in the history of symbols. W. H. Auden in

The Enchafed Flood describes both the romantic and the older uses of the sea voyage as a symbol. He characterizes the romantic symbol as follows:

1. To leave the land and the city is the desire of every man of sensibility and honour.
2. The sea is the real situation and the voyage is the true condition of man. . . .
3. The sea is where the decisive events, the moments of eternal choice, of temptation, fall and redemption occur. The shore life is always trivial.
4. An abiding destination is unknown, even if it may exist: a lasting relationship is not possible nor even to be desired.

With this he contrasts the older meaning of the symbol:

The putting to sea, the wandering . . . is a pain which must be accepted as a cure, a death that leads to rebirth.[19]

Clearly the Mariner's voyage partakes of both these senses, but it is interesting that Coleridge would already have met a quite formal statement of the older, biblical interpretation of the allegory of a sea voyage not long before he wrote the poem. At some time before he wrote *Kubla Khan,* and so presumably in 1797, Coleridge read Wordsworth's copy of *Purchas his Pilgrimes,* and early in the book he would have seen an account of "The Allegoricall and Anagogicall sense or application of SOLOMONS Ophirian navigation":

For the naturall man, that abides at home in him-selfe, and hath not travelled from his owne Wisdome and Selfe-conceite, *knows not the things of God,* nor the *greate Mysteries of Godlinesse;* he must leave the Land, his *Earthly Wisdome* (Terraque urbesque recedant) and *launch into the deepe,* there having sayles filled with the winde, the illumination of that Spirit, which leads unto all truth. . .[20]

For all its simplicity, this passage is very close to the experience which the Mariner's voyage seems to express, and it does parallel very interestingly one feature of the construction of the poem, the contrast between the everyday (if Gothic) world which the Mariner leaves and returns to, and the deep on which he learns a different wisdom. Despite the kirk of the moral, and the hermit who must shrive the Mariner on his return, the two worlds of the poem are very sharply distinguished, setting historical period and community—the "naturall" in Purchas's sense—against timelessness, isolation, God, and the forces of "nature" in Coleridge's sense.

This passage would have found its way into Coleridge's store of associations. It hardly needs saying that the creation of a great and moving poem is never at any time a matter of finding a prose content and then finding symbols to express it. Rather Coleridge's mind was filled with ways of thinking, leading ideas, images, and significances, which shaped the story as it developed. A condition of this development was that the poem be freed from the limitation of even that attachment to place and circumstance to be found in the Conversation Poems. The three great poems of 1797–98 were presented either as poetic reverie or as Gothic narrative or as both, and the effect was to release them from the demands of realism or even commonsense: Coleridge could develop his material as his feelings and ideas emerged from it.

Wordsworth had already suggested a plot which would bring these into play.

> I myself suggested, for example, some crime was to be committed which should bring upon the Old Navigator, as Coleridge afterwards delighted to call him, the spectral persecution, as a consequence of that crime, and his own wanderings. I had been reading in Shelvock's *Voyages* . . . (of) Albatrosses. . . . "Suppose" said I, "you represent him as having killed one of these birds on entering the South Sea, and that the tutelary Spirits of these regions take upon them to avenge the crime." I also suggested the navigation of the ship by the dead men.[21]

The Old Navigator is obviously one of Wordsworth's solitaries, a man who has to come to his own understanding of the world. Wordsworth and Coleridge were both at this time interested in the effects upon the victim of a curse, and they were also both interested in the healing powers of nature, while Coleridge had also the apocalyptic story, which could be the medium for the expression of his neurotic feelings of guilt and also, in the millennial paradise, an escape from them. Hence in the poem, though there are some things (of which the curse is one) which are never quite resolved or integrated, yet in the main nature with her Wordsworthian "severer interventions," "fostering by fear," and her power as healing nature, works hand in hand with the days of wrath, the resurrection of the dead and the millennial paradise behind the imagery of the poem. It is all the more convincing because Coleridge is dealing not with the history of this world but with the states of an individual soul, and he stops the poem before the point after the last trump corresponding with the end of this world. The curse returns and the Mariner goes back to everyday life to relive his experience.

The form of the poem is framed by the land scenes at beginning and end and between these it is controlled by two large structural patterns; the geographical pattern of the ship's voyage and the pattern of the apocalypse story. The ship's voyage, first to the Antarctic, through the Pacific to the tropics, and then through temperate seas to return home, can be traced on the globe (so long as one remembers that the poem is "medieval" and that in the Middle Ages America did not exist). Here the nature symbolism is an expression of the "Wordsworthian" religion of nature (though Coleridge had as much right as Wordsworth to the naming of it). In these terms *The Ancient Mariner* is a companion piece to *Tintern Abbey,* a poem about the educative power of nature and about the power of imagination to see the life and goodness in the natural world and to respond to it with true feeling. Here the Mariner's distemper lies in his lack of imagination and his icy callousness to other life—in short, in his inability to see the world truly and to respond truly to it. His cure, brought about by nature's severer interventions, is a change in his way of seeing from unimaginative to imaginative; the loathsome creatures of the stifling calm have been replaced by the watersnakes that the Mariner loves for their beauty—what changes is the Mariner's perception of the world. The world which the Mariner sees imaginatively in the late part of the poem is that spiritual universe of life which was Wordsworth's vision also—a world moved by spirit and full of song and rejoicing. From the watersnakes on the moonlit sea to the singing filling the air from ocean to sun, the poem here is a great paean to the beauty and beneficence of the natural world; and the moral here is the "official" one, "He prayeth best who loveth best / All creatures great and small." If this seems a relatively easy and optimistic end to the Mariner's suffering, it does not actually contradict the more sombre apocalyptic account that blends with it. For Coleridge, the God discovered in the beauty of nature was never different from the God discovered in Scripture and inner feeling, and the "family of Love" could be found in either way.

The second controlling structure is the pattern of the apocalypse, partly as modified by Burnet's account. The poem is not a literal retelling of the story but a use of the pattern and of many of its details. It is a mimesis of the last days, with the rotting ocean, the sun red through Burnet's volcanic mist ("all in a hot and copper sky"), the deaths from burning heat, the death-fires, and the water the colour of blood; then the millennial paradise with the mimesis of the first rising of the dead, the millennial breezes, the spirits (whatever their natural basis), and the singing in heaven; and finally the last trump and the sea giving up its dead, at which point the mimesis ends. What should follow is the last judgment, but there is no judgment and no finality in this form of the pattern. It is all, of course, a mimicking, not a direct imitation, and follows not so much Saint John as the pattern of his story: the images (many of which Coleridge had used before in more literal ways) are used here to give a pattern of emotion, a psychic history, expressing grace where the parallel natural imagery expressed imaginative vision. As Coleridge was to write later, states of mind cannot be expressed save through images of time and space,[22] and these were pre-eminently the images for Coleridge's deep fears and hopes.

Many of Saint John's images had been modified by Coleridge in the course of his reading about the apocalypse. A good example of this is the rotting ocean. This is not explicit in Revelation, but Thomas Burnet wrote in *The Sacred Theory of the Earth*, his 'scientific' account of the last days:

> The great Force of the Sea will be broken, and the mighty Ocean reduc'd to a standing Pool of putrid waters, without vent and without recruits. But there will remain in the midst of the Channel a great Mass of troubled Liquors, like dregs in the bottom of the vessel; which will not be drunk up till the Earth be all on Fire.[23]

Among the agents producing this were to be the fiery volcanic whirl-winds of which Coleridge wrote in *Religious Musings*. Coleridge rum-maged a great deal in that storehouse of remarkable facts, the poetry of Erasmus Darwin (who also believed in the millennium though he was thinking of a secular event to be brought about by scientific advances); and one of Darwin's notes had an account of the Harmattan, which he thought was a volcanic wind. In his account the heat of the Harmattan concentrated the salt ocean, killing the fish so that their putrefaction became pestilential, and he suggested in other passages that such pu-trefaction was the cause of the phosphorescence of the tropical seas.[24] In *The Ancient Mariner* all this became:

> The very deep did rot: O Christ!
>   That ever this should be!
> Yea, slimy things did crawl with legs
>   Upon the slimy sea.
>
> About, about, in reel and rout
>   The death-fires danced at night;
> The water, like a witch's oils,
>   Burnt green, and blue and white.[25]

Another part of Darwin's note, describing how a ship caught in such phosphorescence seemed at night to be surrounded by fire, would have blended with the apocalyptic sea turned to blood to produce:

> But where the ship's huge shadow lay,
> The charmed water burnt alway
>   A still and awful red.[26]

The images in this part of the poem have a tremendous resonance because they recall in form and language the images and words which in the Christian tradition have symbolized God's wrath and men's guilt. Such a resonance does not need the reader's recognition to have its effect. A case which illustrates this point can be seen in Shakespeare in Cleopatra's speech when she is preparing for death and immortality; she calls for her robe and crown and speaks, rather oddly, of no longer moistening her lip with the juice of the grape. The pathos and dignity of the speech owe much to the unnoticed echoes of Christ's words at the Last Supper, "I will drink no more of the fruit of the vine," and to the robe and the crown of the Crucifixion, all deeply moving symbols of death leading to immortality.[27] Biblical reference does not need to be explicit to do its work and it does not easily lose its associations and overtones. Coleridge was, in this part of the poem, re-creating symbols of terror and guilt that have long haunted the Western imagination.

The question has often been raised as to whether the killing of the albatross justifies such feelings. Certainly the killing shows callousness towards the beautiful living forms of nature, but it is useless to discuss whether or not it is trivial and whether or not it warrants the punishment. It is unarguable as "once upon a time"; when Wordsworth suggested it, the starting point of the poem became that this was a crime warranting punishment, and the reader takes it as a "given." What Coleridge does supply is the *intensity* of the guilt. But though the Mariner is punished by the Tutelary Spirit and the forces of nature, these do not pronounce sentence on the Mariner. That is brought with the ghost ship, a terrifying visitant from the Gothic world that frames the poem. For all the vividness with which they are delineated, these images of nightmare are not easy to place in any symbolic scheme, but certainly the arbitrary dicing for men's souls must, to one brought up in childhood in the doctrines of arbitrary predestination and eternal damnation, have carried a weight of horror. The sentence is followed by the curse of the dying seamen: those men in Revelation who died because of the intense heat cursed God who sent it; these men curse the man whose guilt brought it and it is an added guilt that the Mariner feels:

> The many men, so beautiful!
> And they all dead did lie:
> And a thousand thousand slimy things
> Lived on; and so did I.[28]

The many deaths had their warrant in Revelation, as did the thirst that, in the "prophetic language," is the symbol of spiritual barrenness.

The Mariner's release from his sufferings is a release into the family of love when he recognizes the beauty of the watersnakes and comes to love them. This change is marked by the biblical symbolism of rain and dew, explained by Newton (if so ancient a symbol needed explanation) as standing for "the graces of the spirit; and the defect thereof for spiritual barrenness."[29] The entry into the family of love was also, as we have seen, the meaning for Coleridge of the millennium, and that now appears as a symbolic representation of the implications of the change. This different response to living beings brings a new, imaginatively known world, and his surroundings are transformed. The horned moon under which the seamen died becomes the moon whose beams suggest hoarfrost and which presides over the life-giving rain; the burning sun becomes the sun to which the singing spirits dart; and the living things seen as slimy shapes are replaced by the happy, living, and beautiful watersnakes. The whole ocean world is transformed and the three large images, after the rain, that express this all have paradisal significance.

The first of these images is a mimesis of the millennial (or first) resurrection of the dead. In the manner of dream images, it is a rising with a difference; the scoffing sailors had been won by death and had no place in this first resurrection to the millennial paradise, but how better can the arrival of paradise be symbolized than by a resurrection. The spirits who animate the bodies seem to have been suggested by natural forces—electrical, metereological, and galvanic—coming from the lightning and the wind to galvanize the corpses; by doing so they announce symbolically the beginning of paradise and the Mariner's own revival. Paradise had been for Coleridge, from his early poetry on, an image or intimation of bliss.

> The massy gates of Paradise are thrown
> Wide open, and forth come in fragments wild
> Sweet echoes of unearthly melodies,
> . . . his silent spirit drinks
> Strange bliss which he shall recognise in heaven.[30]

With this paradisal joy Coleridge habitually associated a cluster of images. There are paradise, soaring, and song in *Joan of Arc*; gentle gales, melodies, and the birds of paradise in "The Eolian Harp"; soft gales, music, and the millennium in *Religious Musings*; song, the upper air, and paradise in *Kubla Khan*. All these images (except the birds who provide the song) have some warrant in biblical descriptions, but the winds seem to owe a good deal to Erasmus Darwin's suggestion that the millennium could be brought about by control of the winds, turning deserts to gardens.[31] Coleridge took the suggestion a little less metaphorically in *Religious Musings*:

> While as to solemn strains,
> The THOUSAND YEARS lead up their mystic dance

> Old OCEAN claps his hands! the DESERT shouts!
> And soft gales wafted from the haunts of spring
> Melt the primaeval North.[32]

In *The Ancient Mariner* these winds are both the preternatural wind, understood in a trance, and the natural breeze that brings the Mariner home. Even the natural breeze has a dreamlike quality:

> Its path was not upon the sea,
>   In ripple or in shade.[33]

And with the preternatural wind, as with the risen dead, there is a clear emphasis on the nature spirits who are the movers. It is not easy to put a symbolic meaning on this other than the Unitarian intuition that God and nature are finally one, but the effect is that, when we come to the singing of the spirits, the poem is both a paradisal rejoicing and a paean to the beauty of nature, which inspires this joy and intuits its divine nature.

> Sometimes a-dropping from the sky
>   I heard the sky-lark sing;
> Sometimes all little birds that are,
> How they seemed to fill the sea and air
>   With their sweet jargoning!
>
> And now 'twas like all instruments,
>   Now like a lonely flute,
> And now it is an angel's song,
>   That makes the heavens be mute.
>
> It ceased; yet still the sails made on
>   A pleasant noise till noon,
> A noise like of a hidden brook
>   In the leafy month of June.[34]

Coleridge thus brought together elements that expressed for him the "Wordsworthian" joy in all living things and the millennial joy of entry into "the family of Love": the quasi-mystical ecstasy that follows the discovery of God in nature and the paradisal joy to be found in the inner consciousness.

Nevertheless, the Mariner himself does not participate in the millennium except through his feelings. Though it is only in the passage dealing with the preternatural action of the air that the Mariner is said to be in a trance, yet in all this part of the poem he is the observer of a vision rather than the actor in it. It all takes place between when he falls asleep after blessing the watersnakes and when he rises, stunned, from the water like one of the dead whom the sea gives up at the last trump. Through it all he sees all but can communicate with nobody:

> The body of my brother's son
> Stood by me knee to knee,
> The body and I pulled at one rope,
> But he said nought to me—[35]

What the Mariner gains is a knowledge of joy, a foretaste of bliss, and not actual participation in paradise himself. Thus it is proper, in the terms which the poem has thus set, that the apocalyptic imagery stops before (indeed immediately before) the last judgment and that, when the Mariner returns to the everyday world, he returns to repeated agony, resolved again into fresh freedom.

Two things mark the end of the Mariner's glimpse of bliss. The first is the curious episode that occurs in the first version when the ship arrives home: the Mariner sees with fear and dread that the corpses have gathered by the mast in the ominous red light burning from their right hands, a light in which their stony eyeballs glitter. William Empson points out the importance of this scene in discussions of the Mariner's "redemption," but there is no need to postulate here, as he does,[36] a struggle of good and bad spirits; nature, and the spirits that represent it, can be benevolent or admonitory by turns, but these are the corpses of the crew, and the look on their faces which haunted the Mariner in the earlier part of the poem has indeed never passed away. He has made no final, permanent escape from guilt.

The second thing is "that loud and dreadful sound" whose resemblance to the last trump has sometimes been noticed. In fact, from its position in the story it is indeed a mimesis of the last trump, marking the end of the millennium and announcing the general resurrection of the dead and the judgment.

> Under the water it rumbled on,
> Still louder and more dread:
> It reach'd the ship, it split the bay;
> The ship went down like lead.

> Stunned by that loud and dreadful sound,
> Which sky and ocean smote,
> Like one that hath been seven days drowned
> My body lay afloat:
> But swift as dreams, myself I found
> Within the Pilot's boat.[37]

The vision of the millennial paradise has ended, but the sea gives up its dead not to the judgment but to everyday life again.

It must be reiterated that Coleridge was not retelling the apocalypse story in disguise, much less writing a theological poem. It is a poem about states of mind, agony and joy, the hell and heaven of life, but the form is appropriate because these are states with which religion is concerned and the ideas and feelings here are those of a religious man, Coleridge himself. What both the religion of nature and the apocalypse story have done is to give shape to the feelings in and about the narrative. The killing of the albatross is simply a starting point, but, to use Wordsworthian phrases, the Mariner's contempt for any living thing shows a lack of that imaginative understanding which cannot be distinguished from love. When he is shut up in his own callousness, he can neither truly see nor truly love; he lives in a world of emblems of his own despair, from which his escape lies into the family of love. Love, vision, and joy come hand in hand and that is the tale he has to tell.

This discussion of the poem has been in terms of three modes or systems of symbolism: the Gothic, nature symbolism and the apocalyptic—which may be thought of as corresponding respectively to the conception of the poem as simple narrative, and then secondly to the idea of the discovery of God in nature, which Coleridge was using, probably more or less consciously, to shape the story, and finally to those elements of feeling which entered from Coleridge's biblical reading and from those perhaps less conscious feelings which, by finding expression here, gave the poem a tone that the "moral" does not account for. Nevertheless, it is obvious that the poem does not exist in layers like a geological deposit. It is rather a matter of the apocalyptic symbolism, which had already become associated with Coleridge's fears and guilts, reaching out to embrace and resolve the ambiguities and contradictions between the world of Coleridge's nightmares and the world of his conscious belief in the goodness of God. *The Ancient Mariner* manages to combine a belief in the goodness of the world with Coleridge's deepest, if you will most neurotic, apprehensions of guilt and suffering, and this tension is embodied in the imaginative experience of the Mariner himself:

> Since then at an uncertain hour,
>   That agony returns:
> And till my ghastly tale is told,
>   This heart within me burns.[38]

The well-known "moral" of the poem,

> He prayeth best who loveth best
>   All things both great and small,

has often been dismissed as too trite to carry the weight of the poem, and so it would be if that were all, but the passage which contains it contains also:

> O Wedding-Guest! This soul hath been
> Alone on a wide wide sea:
> So lonely 'twas, that God himself
> Scarce seemed there to be.[39]

In view of the whole poem, the Mariner's last words are more surprising than they at first seem:

> For the dear God who loveth us,
> He made and loveth all.[40]

The tale certainly shows that God loved the albatross; what is strange is that he also loved the Mariner. The Revelation of Saint John was written at a time of persecution (probably Domitian's) to strengthen the resolve of the martyrs, and there is very little in it (as D. H. Lawrence pointed out very forcefully in his *Apocalypse*)[41] about God's mercy and kindness to that bulk of mankind who formed the persecutors. If Saint John's book is taken literally as future history, then it is chiefly a story of appalling vengeance; but if it is taken as an allegory of the individual soul, then it becomes not only, as Lawrence suggested, an initiation story of entry into new life but also a story of redemption, of the soul plucked out from suffering and death and raised again in paradise. Compared with the Conversation Poems, *The Ancient Mariner* shows, along with that somber sense of agony that was only a pace behind Coleridge, a heightened power to express blessedness and grace and a more vivid re-creation of the moods of creativeness and love. This is all the more powerful because the misery has not been ignored: the joy and beauty have been brought out of suffering by imaginative love.

As Wordsworth showed, the way taken by *The Ancient Mariner* was not the only way Coleridge could have chosen for the poetic treatment of suffering. Wordsworth's "reply," *Peter Bell*, is tame but his real equivalent for the Mariner is any one of his great solitaries,

> About the weary moors continually
> Wandering about alone and silently.[42]

For Wordsworth the consolation came from their human dignity as "natural beings in the strength of Nature,"[43] but this note was outside Coleridge's range. Wordsworth had a temperament of settled happiness that enabled him to look through suffering and loneliness to find sources of strength. Coleridge's life was an alternation of suffering and joy, of which his opium habit was perhaps at first as much an attempted remedy as it later became a cause; and it is this central part of his emotional experience that has gone into the poem. *The Ancient Mariner* is not a theological poem, it uses the last things only as symbolism, and the Mariner returns from the paradisal state with only a knowledge that such a state is possible. Nevertheless, by using the shape and the transformed imagery of the apocalypse, Coleridge created his own myth expressing the experience of love as the way of escape from isolation and suffering to joy, and it is this which makes it one of those great, enduring poems that for the ordinary reader need no analysis.

4
Paradisal Symbolism in *Kubla Khan*

T HE purpose of discussing *Kubla Khan* after and not before *The Ancient Mariner* is simply convenience. There seems no good reason to doubt its traditional dating in the autumn of 1797, just before the conception of the later poem with which its imagery is clearly linked. At a later date, in a note which has produced confusion, Coleridge seems to have conflated two separate visits to a cottage near Porlock; the first visit in 1797 involved an indulgence in opium and the composition of this poem and the second in late 1799, discovered by Elizabeth Schneider,[1] was connected with Coleridge's quarrel with Lamb and what he always regarded as the real start of his opium addiction (as opposed to occasional uses). Dorothy Wordsworth's oblique reference to the poem in 1798[2] shows that it must have been composed before the second occasion. The common link must have been the taking of opium. Nevertheless, there is good reason for discussing this poem second in the order of exposition because the paradisal imagery, which has always been recognized as a major feature of *Kubla Khan*, is in origin one part of the whole system of biblical imagery that informs the longer poem. When Coleridge wrote that,

> All the images rose up before him as *things,* with a parallel production of the correspondent expressions, without any sensation or consciousness of effort,[3]

the remark rings true because the images that arose were elements of the symbolism of paradise with which he had been familiar for some years: the poem arose out of the confluence of a sentence from *Purchas his Pilgrimage* with Coleridge's long study of the paradise story and with the store of images that had already been built up in his mind. Coleridge sent a copy of the poem to the poet "Perdita" Robinson in 1800; we cannot know how much help he gave her with its interpretation (though he surely must have given her some hint), but certainly when she wrote a poem in reply, in October of that year, she treated *Kubla Khan* as entirely a poem about "NEW PARADISE" and even fastened on one important feature of the second paradise when she called the dome "thy TEMPLE."[4] The weight of paradisal reference was noticed again early in this century and has been regularly commented on, but perhaps never fully brought out.

Coleridge was slow to publish the poem, and when he did so he surrounded it with mystifications—that it had been written in a dream, that it was a fragment from a forgotten poem, that he presented it only as a psychological curiosity. All this flurry of explanations represents something more than Coleridge's habitual "quizzing." Coleridge's difficulty was that his meditation on Kubla's garden and the garden of paradise was not conducted in either narrative or discursive terms. Of course it is possible to accept Coleridge's stories and give, as Elizabeth Schneider does,[5] a straightforward account of the poem as a fragment but, though such an account cannot be proved wrong, it is unsatisfying. It does not account for the almost general feeling among critics that the poem is complete, that its motifs are worked out, and that it is shaped as a whole. Feeling rightly that the sense must be similarly complete, most modern critics treat the poem as if it were a modern symbolist poem which can be explained by explicating the symbols, but this still leaves a twofold problem—that Coleridge lived long before the Symbolist school and Symbolist theory, and that they are without any scheme to account for and relate the symbols. They are without a guide and there are as many guesses as critics.

In fact the poem can be seen readily enough as a meditation of paradise, working (because paradise as described is a symbol) in symbols, and the obvious guide to the poem is paradise itself. It had been a symbol long before Coleridge wrote and, as one Catholic encyclopedia remarks, the language in which it is described has always been understood as symbolical.[6] It was a complex symbol in which each of its geographic parts could have its own symbolic significance. Coleridge acquired his knowledge of it from a number of fairly obvious sources. The most important was Milton's description of the primal paradise in Book 4 of *Paradise Lost* and of the fallen Jerusalem in Book 1, the future site of the New Jerusalem or paradise restored, but then haunted by the demons who frequented both Mount Zion and the gorge beside it, the Valley of Hinnom or Lamentation. He also knew the source of this tradition in Ezekiel's description of the restored temple and Saint John's of the New Jerusalem. He had read Burnet's *The Sacred Theory of the Earth*, where he was particularly attracted by the descriptions of the mountains and the caverns that were formed (on this theory) after the fall and the ruin of paradise. There were other possible, if minor, sources and, in addition, in mid-1796 he drew Boyd's 1785 translation of Dante from the Bristol Library, but that contained only the *Inferno*.[7] Still, there is enough in what he certainly knew to provide the pattern of paradise.

This pattern was based on the geography of Jerusalem. When Ezekiel prophesied the restored Jerusalem, his prophecy centered on the restored temple, which was to be built, not on the site of the old temple but on David's hill, Mount Zion, which is the southernmost hill of the city. From the altar of the temple a stream ran out on the south side, that is, down the Valley of Lamentation, which bounded the mount and which was the scene in the Old Testament of the worship of Moloch and Astarte. From here the river, bordered by mystical trees, flowed east to the Dead Sea, where, in a kind of harrowing of hell, it brought life to some but not all of the waters. This picture was the basis of Saint John's account, though he placed the temple in the heavens, turned the spring into the divine fountain Alpha and Omega, and described the Dead Sea, in its capacity of "th'asphaltic pool," as the lake burning with fire and brimstone.[8]

This was the second paradise but as well there was the first paradise, located, according to the ideas of Junius and Grotius[9] that were followed by Milton, on Mount Mazius in Assyria—this mountain is a common source of the Euphrates, its tributary the Chabora or Abora (the Gihon), the Tigris, and its tributary the Pasitigris (the Phison); the four rivers of Eden. This paradise had in Genesis no mountain and no fountain, yet the tradition that the second paradise was a restoration of the primal paradise led to an assimilation of their features.

> We think that *Paradise* and *Calvarie*,
> Christs Crosse and Adams tree, stood in one place.[10]

Thus the primal paradise received both a mountain and a fountain. On the other hand its four rivers could not, obviously, flow to the Dead Sea and instead watered the whole ancient world.

Of course what counts in such symbolism is pattern, and the features can be rearranged to give subtly different meanings or emphases, but the tradition was so strong that Dante, describing the earthly paradise of the redeemed, and Milton, describing the primal paradise, use the same geographical (and symbolical) features, with the exception of the Dead Sea, which cannot appear before death enters the world. At the same time the description is so varied that it is only through pattern that one can realize that these features are the same. In Dante there is one fountain giving rise to two rivers (as in the prophecy of Zechariah)[11] and one of these rivers, Lethe, runs down the mountain and then through a fissure and a cavern down to hell, carrying with it the memory of sins.[12] In Milton the waters from the fountain unite in a single river that falls down the south side of the mountain. In Dante the wall of paradise is placed well down the mountain, and the valley in the mountain outside the wall is the Valley of the Princes, where the serpent daily tries to enter and where he is daily repulsed by the guardian angels. Milton's steep wilderness with hairy sides, through which Satan first enters paradise, is a much less pleasant place and the river does not flow through the valley. Coleridge got his chasm from Milton's valley, as the borrowings show. That in his case it corresponds with the Valley of Lamentation is indicated by the wailing woman, the implied demon-worship, and by the fact that this is where Ezekiel's river is to flow.

There was one feature of *Kubla Khan* which is paradisal and yet not in the biblical accounts and this is Mount Abora. It owes its existence to a seventeenth-century misreading of Ptolemy preserved in a volume of biblical geography available to Coleridge in the Bristol Library. The well-known classical river the Abora (or Chabora with a *chi* or, in the Bible, Habor, or, on modern maps, the Khabur), which had its source in Mount Mazius, had been identified by Junius as the river which watered the fields of Eden.[13] In the texts of Ptolemy, which at one time had no breathing marks for aspirates, the watershed (*horos*) of the Chabora was read as mount (*oros*) Chabora, and Mount Abora duly appeared in Bochartus's *Geographia Sacra*.[14] It was thus an alternative name for Mount Mazius, the site of the primal paradise.

All this is not to suggest that Coleridge either consciously or unconsciously kept tally of the varying accounts (though, as he said, he had studied the subject deeply and widely).[15] Nevertheless, they were all available to him and would have helped to form the pattern of paradisal reference—and it was pattern and reference that were important. It is clear from the varying accounts which the tradition was able to absorb, and from the manipulation that had already taken place, that all this was not geography but symbolic meaning, a way of thinking about or contemplating the paradisal bliss. For the purposes of reference, what was important in this symbolism was pattern, analogy, and application, and from this point of view there is the one pattern, with significant variations, running through the three states of the primal paradise, the fallen Jerusalem, and paradise restored. The variations have special self-evident meaning in distinguishing these states. Such variations are the difference between the primal mountain and Mount Zion, the presence of the Dead Sea, the demons or fallen angels profaning the fallen Jerusalem (the Valley of Lamentation was particularly a place of abomination), and the vision of the Temple.

What might well have triggered the poem was Purchas's use of the word "pleasure" in Kubla's pleasure-dome, for "pleasure" is the literal meaning of "Eden" and this was so well-known that Milton punned on it.[16] Certainly the first part of the poem consists of two sentences drawn from Purchas, each separated, by a colon that has no grammatical function, from a mass of descriptive material all associated with Eden. The landscape that thus thrusts itself into Purchas's passage on Xanadu and shapes the first part of the poem is based on the pattern of the hill, the fountain, the valley or ravine, the river with its trees, and the Dead Sea—with two displacements, for the fountain is in the ravine rather than on the summit, and the river reaches the sunless sea through immeasurable caverns. Geographically this is like Dante's river descending through the cavern to hell in the last canto of the *Inferno*, but these caverns in the plural seem to recall Coleridge's fascination with Burnet, in whose account the original earthly paradise (which in his theory covered the whole earth and had neither rivers nor mountains) collapsed over the original underlying subterranean ocean, producing, along with the present surface of the globe, huge caverns under the earth. Though the sunless sea is not described until later in the poem as a lifeless ocean, its presence here, like that of the caverns, indicates that, if Kubla decreed his pleasure-dome in an Edenic place, then it was Eden after the fall.

What follows the next snippet from Purchas is a description that contains the well-known reminiscences of Milton's paradise. The "gardens bright with many a sinuous rill" recall Milton's "with many a rill / Watered the garden," and the incense-bearing trees reflect the "Groves whose rich trees wept odorous Gumms and Baum" (for incense is an odorous gum), while the forests recall the trees of Eden. But at this point there is a turn, and these suggestions of paradise are undercut by the next sentence with its opening "But," its change in the movement of the verse from end-stopped to overrun, and its change of tone. The "deep, romantic chasm which slanted / Down the green hill athwart a cedarn cover" also has its Miltonic reminiscence, but it is of the valley by which Satan entered paradise, a "steep wilderness, whose hairie sides / With thicket overgrown, grottesque and wild," were topped by the shade of "Cedar and Pine and Fir," and which is later described as "savage," below the "enclosure green" and "rural mound" of paradise.[17] The poem, then, is developing into a meditation not only on paradise but also on what threatens it.

The demon lover and the wailing woman are part of this change, for they too had for Coleridge their apocalyptic associations: in a part of *Religious Musings* dealing with the last days he had described the Great Whore of Revelation as "She that worked whoredom with the Daemon Power,"[18] though there is no demon in this part of the biblical text. The only women in the Bible who wail for a demon are the women wailing for Tammuz seen by Ezekiel in his vision of the abominations of Jerusalem and described by Milton in the first book of *Paradise Lost:*

> The love-tale
> Infected *Sions* daughters with like heat,
> Whose wanton passions in the sacred porch
> *Ezekiel* saw.[19]

But if whoredom with a demon was specially chosen by Coleridge as an abomination marking the fallen world—and it is certainly an evocative one—what still needs explaining is the curious romantic tone of the whole passage, caught up in the strange antithetical phrase "holy and enchanted."

This antithesis has given rise to contradictory interpretations. J. B. Beer takes the scene to represent the demonic sublime and the fountain to be "an image of that which replaces human life—the distortion of angelic energies into demonic," while G. Yarlott on the contrary regards the scene as representative of the vital Gothic or romantic art which was replacing the effete classicism of Kubla's dome:[20] one might say that for Beer the enchantment is that of Comus while for Yarlott the holiness is that of Sir Bedivere's mere and the vale of Avalon. Given a context shot through with biblical and Miltonic references, Beer is likely to be nearer the mark: even at the end of the eighteenth century it is necessary to be cautious about the extent of approval implied by "romantic" and "savage," particularly with Milton's "grottesque" and "savage" somewhere behind the words. Nevertheless, there is a real antithesis here, with both "holy" and "enchanted" to be given their full force.

"Holy" can mean either that the place is holy from a romantic viewpoint, in which case the enchantment and the woman wailing for her demon lover are part of the holiness (and such an attitude would be very possible for later nineteenth-century romanticism); or that the place is holy in the ordinary Christian sense and that it is also enchanted and haunted. In this second case the holiness does not reside in the savagery of the scene: it is holy for the same reason that the river is sacred, because it is part of the site of paradise lost and to come, and it is enchanted (with associations of sorcery) because it is disguised, savage, and haunted by a woman who wails for a demon. (It was Milton's theme in his catalogue of the fallen angels that the demons haunted both Mount Zion and the gorge below it.) The first reading may seem the easier and more natural until we realize that the text is far too early in the history of English romanticism for this, and that such a reading implies that Coleridge was subconsciously of the devil's party or that he was quite frivolous in his use of the word "holy." The second reading, though more complicated, fits the paradisal theme, makes the symbolism more coherent, and is far more possible for Coleridge.

If we adopt this second reading, what still needs to be explained is the tone of the passage. In *Religious Musings* "whoredom with the Daemon Power" is part of a contemporary political and polemical context. Here it is something much more attractive and yet it can be paralleled without moving into nineteenth-century romanticism. The feeling here is very like that other "romantic" side of Milton which emerged when he was writing of the ancient idolatries—the feeling of the "Nativity Ode":

> The lonely mountains ore,
> And the resounding shore,
>   A voice of weeping heard and loud lament:
> From haunted spring and dale.[21]

and of parts of the first book of *Paradise Lost:*

> *Astarte,* Queen of Heav'n with crescent Horns;
> To whose bright Image nightly by the Moon
> *Sidonian* Virgins paid their vows and songs.[22]

These are parallels of tone, not sources, but they bring out the point that this tone is something different from a mere romantic fascination with evil and savageness. In Coleridge it marked an imaginative vision of the fallen world in which the evil is strange, ancient, passionate, and full of its own mystery, but in which the divine is also mysteriously present in the sacred river and the fountain.

In Coleridge's earlier poetry the fountain is his most impressive symbol of the Deity, "the immeasurable fount,"[23] the original of which must be the divine fountain, Alpha and Omega, of Revelation, though Coleridge then placed it in the present heaven. The fountain which appears on earth in the earlier poetry is the "livid fount"[24] belonging to the apocalyptic scheme Coleridge had developed from Burnet and Erasmus Darwin, in which volcanic eruptions were to usher in the last days; and hence it too was a manifestation of the Divine Power. That fountain appears to be a geyser. (Both Burnet and Darwin stressed the geyser's volcanic nature and immense power.)[25] In *Kubla Khan* the two symbols of Divine Power seem to have merged in the landscape of the fallen Eden, for the fountain of this poem is unquestionably volcanic, hurling rocks, shaking the earth, and rising in "half-intermitted burst", but it is also the divine fountain of Revelation for it is the source of the sacred river.

Indeed the mysterious name of that river, Alph, is less likely to be a contraction of Alpheus, which was not a sacred river, than of the Alpha of Alpha and Omega, the beginning and the end, the name of the fountain of water of life.

The river descends to the lifeless ocean, just as the divine river descends to the Dead Sea, and this in the pattern of the New Jerusalem represents the judgment and the second death, and in the tumult of its descent Kubla hears the voices prophesying war—always in the apocalyptic prophecies one of the chief manifestations of God's judgment of the world. Why these should be ancestral voices it is impossible to say: the prophetic voices were ancestral to the Hebrews to whom such prophecies were addressed, and they might be said to be so in a figurative way to Christians, but they could be so to Kubla only through his adoption into a poem filled with Hebrew and Christian symbolism. But, however that may be, Kubla learns at the end of this exposition of the landscape that he has built his paradise on earth in a world where destruction is prophesied. Nevertheless, in the symmetrical center of this passage the motif of Milton's paradise recurs as the river meanders with a mazy motion through wood and dale. In this fallen world runs the river of the water of life.

Thus the first eleven lines consist of four lines drawn from Purchas set into a landscape drawn from the paradisal tradition. Lines twelve to thirty then expand this paradisal material, but at that point the poem returns to the pleasure-dome and brings it into relation with river, fountain, and caves. The passage that follows has a touch of surrealism that makes any interpretation speculative, but something may be attempted by examining the symbolic or allegoric significances of these paradisal images. The relation is first made through the shadow of the dome of pleasure floating on the water: the connection is oblique and is not made easier to interpret by the ambiguity of the word "shadow." The lines have been taken to mean that a second spectral dome was floating midway between the banks;[26] the solid-seeming caves of ice are no absolute bar to this for, after all, the visionary temple which Saint John saw in the heavens contained a sea of glass,[27] but there seems no real need or reason to introduce this specter dome. The logical sense of the lines is that the dome was alongside the river in the middle of its course, so that its shadow or reflection could be seen on the surface of the water, perhaps with patches of clear or gleaming water to suggest the ice. The relationship is an immaterial one and the two entities do not react physically, but in this relationship it is the water which supports the immaterial aspect of the pleasure-dome; in this place the roar of the divine fountain and the tumult full of prophetic and threatening voices have become a harmony, a mingled measure. Allegorically this is very close to a statement that human pleasure floats spiritually on the river of the water of life and is very close to Coleridge's conception of "Joy that ne'er was given / Save to the pure, and in their purest hour."[28] In such a state of grace the divine power and the divine judgment have become a music.

The first part of the next sentence is even more complex: the phrase "a miracle of rare device" is a paradox, for devices are human but miracles divine. Either part could be an intensive, so that the phrase could mean either "a very ingenious device" or "a very intricate miracle," but if both are taken together then the phrase is the announcement of an even more intimate collaboration of the human and the divine. The phrase which fulfils that announcement embodies a symbol of such strangeness and intense poetical power that it has always been the most difficult crux of the poem. Physically the image enacts a reconciliation of opposites, the natural with the manmade, warmth with cold, convexity with concavity. (This is so even though the dome was not necessarily, or even probably, hemispherical: the leading sense of the word in the eighteenth century, strongly reinforced by Pope's *Homer*, which included many phrases like "Erechtheus' sacred dome" for the Erechtheum, was that of a large building or a temple. Wordsworth used the word for Hawkshead School, for ruined abbeys, and for large London houses; indeed, in "Perdita" Robinson's poem, the pleasure-dome was described in imagery drawn from Pope's description of the dome of Alcinous, certainly not a hemisphere.)[29] Yet, though the image enacts a reconciliation, we must look to the symbolism to see *what* has been reconciled. Of the symbols with which the poem began in its first sentence, the dome has already been brought into relation with the sacred river, that is, in symbolic terms, with the river of the water of life; what remains are the caverns measureless to man and the sunless sea. For reasons of poetical economy, the caves of ice must have some analogy with the caves of two lines before, and hence with the caverns of the first sentence. The two sets of caves correspond, but with a difference; these caves which form part of the dome must clearly be measurable to man, and the water which they contain is in the form of ice. They are images, but changed images, of the measureless caverns and the sunless sea. By a miracle the terrifying apocalyptic symbols of judgment and death are emblematically circumscribed and caught up in the sunny pleasure dome, just as, where the water of life and the shadow of the dome touch, the tumult of fountain and caves becomes a harmony, and, in Saint John, the water of life gives everlasting life.[30] Beyond this one cannot go. Thinking in symbols has its own logic and produces its own meanings; these cannot easily be translated into the meanings of philosophy or theology, but they nevertheless can offer insights of value.

At this point the poem has, so to speak, reached the end of a movement. The themes announced in the first sentence have all been worked out and the feelings latent in them brought to their highest intensity, so that now the demands of poetic form lead us to expect a change—either a new development, a new explication, or a repetition in another mode. This second part of the poem is something of all three, and in particular it says something of the two paradises—the memory of the First Paradise and the vision of the Second—that lie on either side of the present world. It begins by introducing a new figure, the damsel who sings of Mount Abora. There is some evidence that Coleridge did associate the river Abora with the river of paradise, as Junius had suggested,[31] and it would be altogether too incredible a coincidence if he introduced Mount Abora here without knowing that it was a name for the mountain of the primal paradise, so that the damsel's song must be taken as another element, and an important one, in the pattern of paradisal reference. The damsel is an ambiguous figure, but the ambiguities are not of the kind which offer two alternative meanings, but rather a matter of opposite suggestions which are eventually resolved. One is the suggestion of the biblical, compounded out of the damsels playing upon timbrels before the sanctuary in Psalm 68, out of the fact that the dulcimer was a biblical instrument (though mentioned only in Daniel, and only in idolatrous worship),[32] and out of the fact that she appears in a vision. (The use of the impersonal construction in the next line probably has no significance except to call further attention to her visionary character.) The other suggestion is of the man-made paradise: the maid is an exotic like Kubla and the word "Abyssinian" connects her with Milton's Mount Amara, the false paradise.[33] One cannot help feeling, too, some correspondence with the wailing woman, whether in contrast or in resolution. The two lines cross when she sings of a mount which could, on these two sets of associations, be either Mount Zion or Mount Amara. The name which first appeared in the surviving manuscript was a hybrid of Amara and Abora—Mount Amora (a name with its own curious implications, particularly in view of the earlier appearance of the wailing woman and of Coleridge's belief that "the dark Passions" can become "Enrobed with Light, and naturalised in Heaven")[34]—but the name which finally emerged in the poem was Mount Abora, the mountain of the primal paradise. The damsel associated with paradise on earth sings of the earthly paradise in Eden.

Though this has been prepared for by the Miltonic echoes in the description of Xanadu, this is the first direct reference to the primal paradise, and the emotion it now arouses is described by the stronger word "delight," a word used earlier by Coleridge in *Religious Musings* in connection with the vision of the millennial paradise. It is the revival of this song of Eden (and of the symphony which recalls the "mingled measure" earlier) that, with the delight that accompanies it, will enable the speaker to build the dome in air. Music, paradise, and the upper air form a constellation in Coleridge's poetry, and that the dome in air is in some way a paradisal vision appears from the conclusion its beholders draw in the last line of the poem. But for the present it is sufficient to remember Saint John's "I looked and, behold, the temple in heaven . . . was opened,"[35] and to note that the dome in air is a similar vision created by a figure whose appearance is, as we shall see, that of an inspired prophet. This assimilation of the pleasure-dome to the temple of paradise is the symbolic resolution of the poem, full of implication for both earthly and divine delight, and the beholders know that what they see is both a creation of magical power and also a vision of religious significance. (The word "beware" curiously straddles both aspects when one remembers its other meaning in Exodus 23:20–21, "Behold, I send an angel. . . . Beware of him and obey his voice.") Certainly they not only try to fence the speaker off with ceremonies of witchcraft but, at the same time, they treat him as a holy and inspired seer who has tasted the milk and honey of the promised paradise.

One reason for this double aspect of the vision is that the speaker who is now introduced is not simply a prophet; he is also a bard in the sense in which the word is used in Thomas Gray's poem, that is to say a *vates* or poet-prophet. The image here is one which goes back to the very early days of Coleridge's poetic career, indeed to his schooldays. In the first version of his "Monody on the Death of Chatterton" he had described the poet in lines which derive directly from Gray's poem "The Bard":

> And whilst Fancy in the air
> Paints him many a vision fair
> His eyes dance rapture and his bosom glows.[36]

In 1794 the bardic figure had become even closer to that in *Kubla Khan:*

> And, as floating in the air,
> Glitter the sunny visions fair.

But Gray's Bard was not simply a poet; he was a poet-prophet. Gray's own note (which Coleridge would have read) to the lines

> (Loose his beard and hoary hair
> Streamed like a meteor to the troubled air)[37]

points the inspiration for the physical appearance of his (and hence of Coleridge's) bardic figure back to Raphael's painting of that archetype of the poet-prophet, Ezekiel, who was the model in more than appearance. Indeed the main difference between Gray's Bard and Ezekiel is the negative one that, where both of them saw visions and prophesied war (like Coleridge in *Religious Musings*), Ezekiel (again like Coleridge in that poem) also prophesied the apocalypse and the New Jerusalem. The figure at the end of *Kubla Khan* is a bard (as opposed to *merely* a poet) because he is also a prophet; what he is to produce is a prophecy, here not in the form of a poem but as a vision in air. Coleridge had shown himself very conscious of his role as a poet-prophet, not only by calling himself "the Watchman" after Ezekiel, but in stressing the sacred character of what he was attempting in poetry.

> I haply journeying my immortal course
> I discipline my young and novice thought
> In ministeries of heart-stirring song,
> And aye on Meditation's heaven-ward wing
> Soaring aloft I breathe the empyreal air.[38]

For Coleridge, as for Ezekiel, writing poetry was the means of conveying the vision, but the end was the vision itself. The interpretation of *Kubla Khan* as a poem about writing poetry has had great success since Maud Bodkin introduced it on quite remarkably impressionistic grounds in 1936,[39] and it at least notices the poet if not the prophet, but it is misdirected. It makes the writing the end and not the means; it gives to the poetic faculty what Coleridge gave to the heavenly vision and robs the poet-prophet of his more important dimension.

That the vision which the prophet builds in air, and which corresponds to the temple in the heavens, is the paradoxical pleasure-dome is striking and important. *Kubla Khan* is a poem about Eden, that is to say, it is a poem about pleasure; and the symbolic statement it makes is a complicated one, encompassing the primal paradise, pleasure in the fallen world, and the second Eden. In the eighteenth century "pleasure," though it had its pejorative senses, was a higher word than it has since become; Coleridge used it to describe the immediate purpose of poetry itself. Nevertheless, pleasure in this poem must be taken as something much wider than religious ecstasy. Kubla is not a divine creator nor even a believer; his dome was decreed for purely human pleasure and was built among the symbols of a fallen world; yet it is set in reminiscences of the primal paradise, is itself a miracle, and could be built again in air by the poet-prophet's paradisal vision. If one were to ask the meaning of the primal paradise, remembering that "all such language was known to be symbolic," then probably one could not do better than to quote Pascal:

This then is the condition in which men are today. There still remains
to them some powerless intuition of the happiness of their original
nature, but they are plunged into the miseries of their blindness and
their concupiscence, which have become their second nature.[40]

When the poem sets symbolically the relations between the pleasure-
dome and the two paradises, it does so infinitely more richly than any
bare paraphrase can suggest; but the main thrust, which sees human
pleasure even in a fallen world as paradoxical and miraculous, a memory
of Eden and a foretaste of paradise, is clear enough. Just as God is the
anonymous object of all desire so all pleasure is an aspect of that divine
joy which Coleridge later called "a new Earth and a new Heaven." The
primal eden, human pleasure, and the paradise to come are all aspects of
the same "strange bliss," the joy that Coleridge was always seeking in a
threatening world.

Coleridge had been experimenting with the "prophetic language" and
thinking about the paradisal vision for some years before he wrote *Kubla
Khan*. So it is not surprising that the imagery, which welled up so
spontaneously, and which Coleridge could manipulate without perhaps
knowing in other terms the meanings he produced, should have come
from this source, nor is it surprising that a reading of the poem in these
terms should sharpen its sense and bring out the coherence of its
symbolism; but it must be recognized that the broad emotional drift of
the symbolism is apparent even on a cursory reading of the poem. That
the pleasure-dome is built in a landscape containing images both of
paradisal beauty watered by the sacred river and of immense power and
strange evil, that destruction is threatened, that the dome of pleasure is
miraculous, and that joy is the means by which vision and paradise can
be achieved, are all apparent on the surface of the poem and can be
applied symbolically to whatever suitable themes we wish. Thus one
critic can find the joy in the writing of poetry, another in romantic
energy, and yet another in sexual experience; and there is nothing except
one's view of the intensity of the joy proposed to make one more suitable
than another. But both the joy and the poetic mission were more deeply
grounded for Coleridge both in his symbolic art and in his religion. He
goes behind and beneath the various examples of joy to make a statement about the nature of joy itself, and a knowledge of the traditional
meanings of the paradisal symbols enables us to appreciate that statement more fully.

Nevertheless, it is natural that the symbolism of the poem should be
capable of wider and vaguer application. *Kubla Khan* differs from, for
instance, *The Ancient Mariner* in that there is no real narrative structure;
there is only the symbolism to give shape and meaning to the poem.

Here the symbols rose unbidden and, as Coleridge was later to say of association generally, it was "the state of feeling" embodied in each of them that associated them, related them, and contrasted them to achieve the "meaning" of the poem. Coleridge's characteristic use of symbolism, so potent for the second generation of romantic poets, and, by its transmission through Poe, so potent for the French Symbolist movement, is to be seen in this poem at the very point of transformation from the old ways of allegorical thought to the new ways of symbolic apprehension.

5
Nature and the Gothic in *Christabel*

THE first part of *Christabel* was written in the spring of 1798, a spring of which we have a record in Dorothy Wordsworth's *Journal* and which contributed much of the nature imagery in this part of the poem. The poem was then laid aside until the middle of 1800, when Coleridge attempted to continue it, but he found great difficulties in this and eventually abandoned the poem at the end of the second part. The two parts were thus separated by his visit to Germany and by the changes in his thought which that visit brought. Thus the two parts were written in different moods and in two very different stages in his thought: the difference between the two parts is the kind of difference found between *Kubla Khan* and "Dejection" (or perhaps even "The Mad Monk; an Ode in Mrs. Ratcliff's Manner"). In view of this it is remarkable that *Christabel* is almost always treated as a single, unified, if unfinished poem, and that critics try to demonstrate, variously, which of the three different endings which Coleridge talked about later was the true one. Wordsworth, who was in some position to know, more than once said firmly that at the end of the first part Coleridge had no definite plan for the poem—"not that he doubted [Coleridge's] sincerity in his assertions to the contrary"[1]— and both he and Lamb disapproved of the attempt to continue it.

The chief differences between the two parts can be outlined briefly. The first part is a comparatively static confrontation of the two figures that invite symbolic interpretation; the second has a great deal of varied action. The first part is set in an unlocalized Gothic world; the second is brought to earth in the detailed topography of Cumberland. The first part is full of ambiguities of situation and character reflected in paradoxical imagery; the second is comparatively unambiguous and its two best images, the divided cliff and the snake coiled round the dove, are straightforward in their relation to the action. (Any ambiguity remaining in the character of Geraldine can only be derived from the first part.)

74

Finally, the first part is without explanations and, if a "meaning" is to be given to it, this must be found in an explanation of the symbolism. The second part has full explanations, of a psychological kind, and is "novelistic" in Northrop Frye's sense. Plainly the second part does not really attempt to retain the essential character of the first part, and the differences are so great that they can only be the reflection of something deeper than a merely mechanical difficulty in sustaining the atmosphere. Criticism of the first part can only gain in coherence, clarity, and depth by leaving the second part aside for entirely separate discussion.

In the *annus mirabilis* of 1797–98 Coleridge's major poems explored ideas or feelings of a religious kind which were important to the poet— paradisal joy in *Kubla Khan*, guilt (however neurotic) and release from it in *The Ancient Mariner*, and permitted evil in *Christabel*. In each of these poems the setting plays a vital part in the working out of the poem. In *Kubla Khan* it provides a symbolic landscape drawn from the already symbolic descriptions of paradise. In *The Ancient Mariner* there is a seascape which alters with the Mariner's state and which is the expression of misery and joy. In the first part of *Christabel* the natural setting is ambiguous, mingling darkness with moonlight and glimmerings, inhabited by the owl and the cock (the birds of darkness and of light), poised between winter and spring, and providing a final chorus in which "a star hath set, a star hath risen," and in which the nightbirds rejoice from wood and fell. These match the ambiguities of the poem itself. The problems of the character of Geraldine, as she shows herself in the two central metaphors of the poem, that of the mother and child and that of the marriage bed, have been much discussed:[2] the more common conclusions drawn, however, have not allowed a great deal of ambiguity in the interpretation of the poem. Where it has not been seen as a story of evil triumphant,[3] it has been seen as an essentially psychological treatment either of sexuality and the transition from childhood to maturity, or of "the psychological borderland where matters of religion overlap with matters of sex."[4] How adequate these conclusions are will be discussed later.

A preliminary question is how far we can trust the symbolic organization of this first part. House concluded that the mystery was produced ad hoc "at point after point . . . by . . . suggestions of slight distortions in behaviour, or of contrast, or of surprise," and that in the end these suggestions are "all fragmentary,"[5] but when the first hundred lines of the poem are examined carefully, it can be seen that the various themes of the poem, the ambiguous setting, and the equally ambiguous suggestions of the mother and the marriage are introduced and orchestrated with care and provided with hints and connections that become fully

apparent only in retrospect. The opening lines of the poem are immediately paradoxical—the birds of night have awoken the bird of day—
and the correspondence and antithesis between midnight and midday is
to play its part in the poem. The following lines link midnight and
mastiff with the mother, and both linkages are to be used later to suggest
some strange identity between the mother and Geraldine. Then comes a
passage which is said in one criticism to "show a tension between what
is expected by the inhabitants of the castle and the reality outside,"[6] but
which it seems better to take simply as the voice of the narrator estab-
lishing the antithetical setting—the night chilly but nearing May, the
moon full but dulled with cloud.

With the appearance of Christabel comes the first hint, in her dream,
of the marriage theme (and with it prayer), but the next emphasis is
again given to the setting, with only parasitic plants green, the broad-
breasted oak bare, and its one leaf a threatened survivor. Christabel
herself is not described, but with the introduction of Geraldine appearance becomes important:

> There she sees a damsel bright,
> Drest in a silken robe of white
> That shadowy in the moonlight shone:
> The neck that made that white robe wan,
> Her stately neck, and arms were bare;
> Her blue-veined feet unsandal'd were,
> And wildly glittered here and there
> The gems entangled in her hair.[7]

There are two immediate links here, muted though they are at this point:
the one between the white robe and the shroud at which the mastiff
howls when only he can see the spirit of the mother (and both Geraldine
and the mother hear the castle bell), and the other link between the
apparition "that shadowy in the moonlight shone" and the glimmerings
that light the setting of the poem.

There is another important aspect of Geraldine's appearance. The
strangeness, the brightness and the shadowiness, the appearance by
moonlight, and the wild glitter of the jewels are warnings that this is no
ordinary mortal, if a mortal at all. In his article "The Quantock
Christabel," J. Adlard has pointed out a number of Somerset superstitions
which indicate that Geraldine comes from the old world of Fairy; among
these indications are her white robe and white palfrey, and the white
horses of her companions.[8] This suggestion seems clearly right, for the
superstition went far beyond Somerset; the Elf-Queens and their atten-
dants in the Scottish ballads rode on milk-white steeds.[9] Indeed the two
women of the poem have come from a version of a Scottish ballad,

Percy's "Sir Cauline" where the contrast between them must have been part of Coleridge's first intuition of the poem. In "Sir Cauline" they are the heroine, Christabelle:

> Fair Christabelle to his chaumber goes
> Her maydens followyng nye[10]

and the lady bright who appears in the moonlight with the Eldritch Knight whom Sir Cauline has to overcome:

> Unto midnight that the moone did rise,
> He walked up and downe . . .
> And soone he spyde on the mores so broad,
> A furyous wyght and fell.
> A ladye bright his brydle led,
> Clad in a fayre kyrtell.[11]

Geraldine's otherworldly appearance comes from the fact that she is, from her origin in the ballad, eldritch, a visitor from the other world of the Elf-Queens; but it should be remembered that eldritch beings, though dangerous to mortals and amoral, are not simply evil, much less vampires.

It is time now to examine the character of Geraldine in relation to the two metaphors of mother and of marriage, and in her relationship with the things of the poem and with its setting. The first point of relationship is made when the mastiff bitch moans at her presence as, we have been told earlier, she moans at "my lady's shroud." "What can ail the mastiff bitch?" Clearly something connected in some way with my lady, the mother. But the chief connections come in the central episode of the poem, when Geraldine can summon the mother with a wish, dismiss her, take her place for an "hour," and be revived by the wine she has prepared. It is as some kind of surrogate for the mother, appointed apparently by "they who live in the upper sky," that Geraldine has her power, and the nature of this power is at the center of the mystery of the poem.

Coleridge had already seen, in reviewing Lewis's novel *The Monk*, that this question of power is central to the moral effect of any Gothic story. He wrote then that a romance, by which he meant a Gothic tale, "is incapable of exemplifying a moral truth. . . . Human prudence can oppose no sufficient shield to the power and cunning of supernatural beings. . . . The praise which a romance can claim is simply that of having given pleasure during its perusal".[12] If Coleridge now himself wrote a Gothic tale, it should be that, despite the supernatural power displayed, or perhaps even because of the nature of that power, there was in it some real moral question. Certainly the power of evil was a difficult moral question for a necessarian like Coleridge, who believed that God was omnific, ultimately responsible for all actions in the world, and that all evil is ultimately subservient to good. It is possible to use this as justifying Bostetter's conclusion (argued chiefly from the second part of the poem) that "Geraldine is an incarnation of sadism," and that "all these characteristics (her shame, dread, love and pity) are quite compatible, with, in fact conducive to, the conception of Geraldine as the instrument used by 'Eternal Strength and Wisdom' to torture and test Christabel for its own inscrutable purposes."[13] But the ambiguity of the poem tells against such a conclusion. Certainly it could be possible to believe, as this implies, that Geraldine's identification with the mother is wholly ironical, but more important than the ease or difficulty of this is that such a view fails to explain Christabel's own reaction to Geraldine's hour. This reaction will be discussed more fully later, but clearly there is enlightenment and joy in it as well as suffering. Geraldine's power does indeed seem to come from above, and Bostetter does state (and perhaps overstate) one side of the question, but it is obviously not the whole.

Christabel's first invitation to the couching, her carrying Geraldine over the threshold, bridegroom-fashion, and her mother's vow that she would hear the bell strike twelve on Christabel's wedding day (and it has just struck twelve midnight)—all indicate that this is in some oblique or metaphorical sense a marriage. Very remarkably it is Geraldine who prays before bedding and Christabel who, it would seem, prays in her sleep afterwards. Some commentators have assumed that Geraldine only pretends to pray, but this is not so in the text: when Christabel turns to look she sees Geraldine bowed before the angel-lamp, and the latter's action in revealing her withered side is described as if it were an action imposed on her by a higher power.

It is easy (and common) to make the assumption that the spell imposed on Christabel by the touch of Geraldine's breast is some knowledge or intuition of sexual experience (and presumably, because the breast is withered and foul of hue, intuition of its disgusting aspects), but this is unlikely. What we have here is not an actual marriage but a metaphor, and that the marriage should be a metaphor for a marriage is too simple a reduction. Christabel marries symbolically with the whole meaning of Geraldine, and Coleridge was surely right to resent strongly the suggestion that Geraldine was simply a man in disguise. Yet this is the final implication of the sexual initiation theories.

These interpretations, and also those which lean towards martyrdom as the explanation of the mystery, look for support from Coleridge's later statement that the original inspiration of the poem might have been Crashaw's poem on Saint Teresa, a poem which is certainly about martyrdom and about sexual union, but both of these have very unusual senses in Crashaw. Saint Teresa did not in fact achieve martyrdom but union with God, and the central image of the poem is the defloration of a virgin as the mystical symbol of that union, a martyrdom of bliss. Now Geraldine is not God and Christabel did not experience that bliss, much less the sexual ecstasy which mystically represents the divine one. But if Crashaw's lines did in any way inspire the first part (and Coleridge's statement was very tentative, the more so when compared with his usual certainty on doubtful matters), then the marriage is a metaphor of union at a high level, and Christabel has become in some sense a sharer in Geraldine's knowledge, experience, and condition, and what follows in Christabel's dream is a consequence of this.

There was in Coleridge's own earlier poem, *The Destiny of Nations*, a martyr-saint in Joan of Arc, whose reaction to a world of sin and suffering is very similar to Christabel's reaction to Geraldine's hour. Joan too dreams with open eyes a fearful dream, and she too weeps and is calmed by knowing her guardian angel near, though she does these things in very much worse verse than Christabel does:

> Ah! suffering to the height of what was suffered,
> Stung with too keen a sympathy, the Maid
> Brooded with moving lips, mute, startful, dark!
> And now her flushed tumultuous features shot
> Such strange vivacity, as fires the eye
> Of Misery fancy-crazed! and now once more
> Naked and void, and fixed, and all within
> The unquiet silence of confused thought
> And shapeless feelings. For a mighty hand
> Was strong upon her. . . .
> Yea, swallowed up in the ominous dream, she sate
> Ghastly as broad-eyed Slumber! a dim anguish
> Breathed from her look! and still with pant and sob,
> Inly she toiled to flee, and still subdued,
> Felt an inevitable Presence near.[14]

Allowing for the difference in the power of the poetry and the subtlety of the insight, this is Christabel's experience in her dream. Whether that open-eyed dream would have led to martyrdom is very doubtful, for Christabel's experience was of something less easily remedied than the state of France. Joan had come to learn the evil in the world through seeing the suffering of war. What Christabel had learned is something whose meaning must be sought in the character of Geraldine.

Geraldine's nature must be seen as distilled from the whole setting of this part of the poem, and thus in turn from what Coleridge intuited in the landscape of his moonlight walks with Dorothy Wordsworth; a landscape of delayed spring, the only green in the brambles and hollies and the moss at the roots of the bare oak which pointed its finger to the clouded moon, the chilly night, the dancing of the withered leaf, and the disturbed nightbirds,[15] all of which he associated with the contrast between the daylight and the moonlight women of "Sir Cauline." Geraldine is the being with whom the natural things of the poem show affinity. She appears mysteriously in the moonlight landscape; fire responds to her ambiguously, the open fire burning bright and the lamp-flame dim; the mastiff and the owls recognize her power in various ways; and when the owls celebrate her hour, they do so from the wide natural landscape, "from cliff and tower . . .from wood and fell." As an eldritch being she is neither human nor nonhuman, and she can be seen as representing the complex, darker-side nature of the setting, though she is still, the metaphors insist, both Mother Nature and the nature which, in Coleridge's phrase from "Dejection," we must wed to us,[16] even if here she brings a more doubtful dower.

As a moral being she shows the same ambiguity, unable to pray to the Virgin and yet able to pray to some more anonymous power, her body disfigured by the marks of shame and sorrow, mingling beauty and foulness, a "mother" who is a worker of harms, bringing a meeting that is the midnight opposite of human marriage and an experience which means that "a star hath set, a star hath risen." She is part of an order ordained in upper sky but, in that order, nature's holy plan is neither simple nor scrutable. The natural world was important to both Wordsworth and Coleridge as at once the symbol and the language of the benevolent God in nature. But what place has either Geraldine or the landscape of this poem in it? Coleridge was in the end optimistic. "In my calmer moments I have the firmest faith that all things work together for good," he wrote, and the owls do awaken the cock, the spring will come, and the saints will aid, "but meanwhile it seems a long and dark process."[17] In his "Wordsworth in the Tropics" (although that essay was quite unfair to Wordsworth), Aldous Huxley remarked that "nature, even in the temperate zone, is always alien and inhuman, and occasionally diabolic";[18] and without going so far, the first part of *Christabel* shows a far less comfortable vision of nature, with far more intuition of the possible evil in it, than was to be found in the Conversation Poems of the period.

This marks a considerable development both of Coleridge's poetic vision of nature and of his approach to the problem of evil. In the Conversation Poems, whose concern after all is encounter with God in nature, nature is wholly benevolent and "no sound is dissonant that tells of life." In *Kubla Khan,* though something darker appears in the chasm, the emphasis is on Paradise and the joy it represents. In *The Ancient Mariner,* the forces of nature are sometimes terrifying and sometimes full of beauty and joy, but always moral in their purposes. In *Christabel* both the natural setting and the character of Geraldine call into question the moral purposes of the natural world and the place of evil. It is a question that has been answered—at least for the great mystics. It was so for Wordsworth, through the mystical ecstasy,

> In which the burthen of the mystery,
> In which the heavy and the weary weight
> Of all this unintelligible world
> Is lightened,[19]

and for Saint John of the Cross:

> He can perform most wondrous labours
> Though good and bad in me are neighbours
> He turns their difference to naught
> Then both into Himself.[20]

Coleridge had experienced a nature ecstasy through finding God in the beauty of nature, though it seems to have been short of the fully mystical experience. So his belief that evil was subservient to good rested still on logical grounds, even if he found the matter difficult. Nevertheless, in this poem he seems to have been struggling towards an emotional understanding of the mystery similar to that achieved by the true mystics. It is unfortunate that his later attempt to continue the poem has obscured the importance of Christabel's dream as the climax of the poem as originally written, and as a response and a potential resolution to its theme. Just as Joan's understanding of suffering is not only a call to martyrdom but an experience that troubles the depth of her being, so Christabel's contact with Geraldine's mystery brings a fearful dream of tears, sudden smiles, vision, and prayer, which only she herself can resolve (though, like Joan, with the help of her guardian spirit). Her task was Coleridge's, to find how to "redeem Nature from the generall curse."[21] Christabel has been compared to Blake's Thel, but what she has to resolve is something more than dawning sexuality. The poem itself has been treated as a reconciliation of opposites, but the opposites are blended in wintry and benighted nature and can only be resolved in Christabel. Unfortunately, the spring episode of *Christabel* was never written.

The problem of continuing *Christabel* was the twofold one of the moral purposes of nature and of just how Christabel's fearful dream "of that alone which is" did also contain joy. The setting in time just before the

advent of spring and the description of Christabel's dreaming, and
indeed the final line affirming that "the blue sky bends over all," imply
that both questions could be answered within the poem and in its own
terms, but when Coleridge came to continue the poem in 1800, he gave
no answers. Indeed he moved away from the difficulties altogether.
Coleridge came to speak later of the "vision" he had of the poem, but
that he had lost that vision he originally had can be seen from the
triviality of the verse when he came to redescribe the dream. Compare:

> Again she saw that bosom old,
> Again she felt that bosom cold,
>
> . . . .
> The touch, the sight, had passed away,
> And in its stead that vision blest,
> Which comforted her after-rest
> While in the lady's arms she lay,
> Had put a rapture in her breast,
> And on her lips and o'er her eyes
> Spread smiles like light![22]

with the movement and particularity of the corresponding passage in
the first part:

>   and tears she sheds—
> Large tears that leave the lashes bright!
> And oft the while she seems to smile
> As infants at a sudden light!
>
> Yea, she doth smile and she doth weep,
> Like a youthful hermitess,
> Beauteous in a wilderness,
> Who, praying always, prays in sleep.[23]

While the later-written description was in unevocative "poetic" language, here there is an organic quality; words and phrases like
"wilderness," "hermitess," "prays," and "sudden light" have implications that reach into other parts of the poem from its early setting to the
guardian spirit. Consistently with this, what is here a deeply mingled
vision became in the later version two separable parts in a conventional
opposition.

   This decline in the quality of the language is obvious throughout the
second part. Certainly the image of the divided cliff deserves its praise as
an emblem of common experience, but most of the other verse that
surrounds Sir Leoline is very ordinary Gothic fustian:

"And if they dare deny the same,
My herald shall appoint a week,
And let the recreant traitors seek
My tourney court—that there and then
I may dislodge their reptile souls
From the bodies and forms of men!"
He spake—his eye in lightning rolls![24]

This is not very different from the stuff of the Gothic romances. Scott did it better.

Nature has little to do with the atmosphere of the second part of the poem. The change to the morning landscape of Cumbria means the complete disappearance of the night scene and the nightbirds that accompanied the eldritch Geraldine. Apart from the lists of place names, there are now only the mountain echoes, providing a simple, indeed comic, devil assisted by three sinful sextons' ghosts. Instead of employing the subtle associations that allowed preternatural power to be supported by the natural setting of the poem, Coleridge now developed the character of Geraldine more directly and, at base, more prosaically. She became a lamia with serpent's eyes, identified with the snake coiled round the dove. Again a simple and unambiguous Gothic effect has been substituted for a much more complex one. For the mechanism of his story Coleridge turned, as he was later to turn in a different way in philosophy, to the powers of the mind. He had long been interested in an aspect of Obi and Copper River Indian witchcraft—the power to cast spells by "workings on the imagination" of the victims—and in "the progress and symptoms of the morbid action on the fancy," and he used this in 1797 in his introduction to "The Three Graves" to explain the effectiveness of the mother's curse in that poem, the merits of which he thought "exclusively psychological."[25] In the second part of *Christabel* he worked this idea out more fully in terms of the heroine's passive imitation of Geraldine's "look of dull and treacherous hate." That "forced unconscious sympathy," robbing her of all her powers, completes her domination by Geraldine. It is indeed a situation of evil triumphant, but that evil is no longer the metaphysical evil it was. At the end of the second part the poem has the makings of a chilling Gothic yarn, but it is no longer the poem that Coleridge started with.

It is difficult to be certain what Coleridge thought in 1800 about the religion of nature, and more particularly about the goodness of nature. Some faltering can be seen in the "Lines written in the Album at Elbingerode" (though that poem did not assume its transcendental form until years later), where the homesick poet found that the beauty of nature did not move him without "One spot with which the heart associates / Holy remembrances."[26] On the other hand in this period he still professed belief in the impulses from "Blest intuitions and communions fleet / With living Nature, in her joys and woes,"[27] and he still trusted to these influences for the education of Hartley. However, Coleridge's conscious beliefs are presumably not the point in question. The poem was never a conscious and discursive statement of belief but rather an intuition that could only be explored in terms of symbolism, and probably even that below the level of conscious art. When Coleridge had lost touch with that intuition he had no means of recapturing it. The poem must have come out of the eerie atmosphere of the delayed spring, the moonlight walks, and the disturbed nightbirds and out of Coleridge's memory of "Sir Cauline" with its daylight heroine evocatively named Christabelle and its eldritch lady bright in the moonlight (even though in the ballad the two did not meet). Coleridge's apprehension of the poetic and symbolic possibilities of these elements led him to a poem which asks its question entirely in symbolic form. The difference between this and the other two great poems of this period is that here he had no symbolic tradition to draw on, and that he developed the symbolism himself out of the *données* of the poem.

His later difficulties then lay less in his conscious creed than in deeper poetic intuitions. What nature held for Coleridge in 1797–98 was the promise of joy. This is the theme of the Conversation Poems of that time. It is also the theme of the three major poems, but one of the marks of their difference is that there is in each of them a recognition of the darker, more threatening aspects of nature. In *Kubla Khan* the threat to joy is resolved away, and paradise restored by miracle and by the power of the poet-prophet. In *The Ancient Mariner* nature needs the covert support of the apocalypse story to bring the Mariner from the days of wrath into a resurrection to joy and to the heavenly music, and it is impossible to say whether the beauty of nature or unaccountable grace is the more important agent in this redemption; but there is never any doubt that nature is moral, that its creatures must be loved, and that it is the bringer and symbol of joy. But in the first part of *Christabel* the night-side of nature is brought fairly under poetic scrutiny and the question which it poses and attempts to answer becomes Tennyson's, in *In Memoriam* 55, "Are God and Nature then at strife / That Nature lends such evil dreams?"

6
Changing Ideas and the "Letter to Asra"

THE period which Coleridge spent in Germany from September 1798 to July 1799 was of great importance to the development of his ideas, even though its full effects were spread over some years after his return to England. The most obvious of these effects was his eventual adoption of German idealist philosophy, learned from a study of Kant and the post-Kantian philosophers; but this was part of an even more important religious change which Coleridge described later to one of his correspondents by giving "an extract from a letter which I wrote a few months ago to a sceptical friend, who had been a Socinian, and of course rested all the evidences of Christianity on miracles":

> I fear that the mode of defending Christianity, adopted. . .by Dr. Paley, has increased the number of infidels;—never could it have been so great, if thinking men had been habitually led to look into their own souls, instead of always looking out, both of themselves, and of their nature. . . . Even as Christ did, so would I teach; that is, build the miracle on the faith, not the faith on the miracle.[1]

In 1799 and 1800 this was still to come, but it is possible to see that the interests which led Coleridge to Germany were both literary and religious. When he began to learn German in 1796 the authors that interested him were Schiller, whose dramatic works he was eventually to translate; Semler and Michaelis, the theologians who pioneered the historical criticism of the Bible; "the most unintelligible Emmanuel Kant," "the great German Metaphysician"; and that "most formidable infidel," Lessing, to whose arguments Coleridge meditated a reply.[2] While he was in Germany some of these interests had to wait while he studied German language and literature and attended lectures in the biological sciences, though he did continue to work on a life of Lessing and brought back German books including the work of Kant.[3]

In 1801 and early 1802 Coleridge began an intensive study of philosophy from Locke to Kant, the most important result of which was that he became convinced that the mind played an active, and not merely a passive, part in the perception of the world. This idea, of course, shows the influence of Kant, for whom the mind was the only interpreter and shaper of all that was knowable in the external world, and perhaps of Fichte, with whose thought he had also been in contact in Germany[4] and for whom there were no external things-in-themselves to be interpreted and for whom the mind made the world. Ideas of this sort soon appeared in Coleridge's letters, and on 23 March 1801 he wrote to Thomas Poole:

> Newton was a mere materialist— *Mind* in his system is always passive—a lazy Looker-on an external world. If the mind be not *passive*, if it be indeed made in God's image, & that too in the sublimest sense— the Image of the *Creator*—there is ground for suspicion, that any system built on the passiveness of the mind must be false, as a system.

Despite the obvious Kantian influence, Coleridge was nevertheless moving in a slightly different direction—a direction that was to be influential both in literature and in religious apologetics—and this difference arose out of Coleridge's long-standing interest in psychology. In Kant the imagination which produced man's primary perception of the external world was a metaphysical power: it is deduced by logic and there is no point in asking *how* it functions. On the other hand, Coleridge's theory was to be based on psychology, no longer the system of Hartley which had been the basis of his earlier thinking, but reminding us how important to him such an approach had always been. Now indeed, "not finding psychological analysis in Kant's book, Coleridge condemns him at first as a 'wretched psychologist.' "[5]

Looking then for a psychological mechanism in this active perception of the world, Coleridge came to the conclusion that the active power which associates ideas in the mind is the mind's state of feeling. He hinted at this as early as September 1800, but it is most clearly set out in a letter to Southey on 7 August 1803:

> I hold, that association depends in a much greater degree on the recurrence of resembling states of Feeling, than on Trains of Idea / that the recollection of early childhood in latest old age depends on, & is explicable by this,—& if this be true, Hartley's System totters.—If I were, asked how it is that very old People remember *visually* only the events of early childhood. . .I should think it a perfectly philosophical answer / that old age remembers childhood by becoming 'a second childhood.'. . . I almost think, that Ideas *never* recall Ideas . . . any

more than Leaves in a forest create each other's motion—The Breeze it is that runs thro' them, it is the Soul the state of Feeling.

Thus in the mind it is the state of feeling which plays the creative role and which is active in shaping and interpreting the world which we perceive.

These two letters show quite clearly the change in his ideas. He had previously believed that God in nature, using nature as his language, impresses himself on men and builds up their feelings in harmony with the forms of nature. He now believed that God the Creator has given man a mind in his image, which is therefore itself able to create the world of nature, and that the feelings play a vital part in this creation. This change in his view of the relationship between God, nature and the mind had a revolutionary effect on his theory of natural symbolism and on his quest for joy. Where previously the divine life in nature, expressed in the beauty of its forms, had healed and harmonised man and brought him back to joy, and now the One Life in nature was an expression of the feelings that were active in its perception, and joy was not the result of communion with nature but was the state of feeling that created the One Life. The divine life in nature now came from the human mind created in the divine image. The consequences of this for natural symbolism were very well put, forty years later, by H. N. Coleridge in his advice to Elizabeth Barrett, "to shoot your own being outwards, so that inanimate nature or alien life shall become a projected self, reflecting back on others, modified and combined, from rock or tree, from dying hero or peasant girl, the emotions, the sympathies which truly spring from *you*."[6] At the same time, though he had almost ceased to use biblical symbolism, Coleridge tried to bring language and ideas into the same scheme. In Hartley's system the association of ideas had been the power which produced complex ideas; now the active power of the creative mind was to be thought of as filling this function, and words might be in this sense something like natural symbols, outgrowths of man's creative power. On 22 September 1800, when he was at the beginning of his new way of thinking, he wrote to Godwin:

I wish you to write a book on the power of words, and the processes by which human feelings form affinities with them—in short, I wish you. . .to solve the great Questions—whether there be reason to hold, that an action bearing all the *semblance* of pre-designing Consciousness may yet be simply organic, & whether a *series* of such actions are possible—. . . Is *thinking* impossible without arbitrary signs? &—how far is the word 'arbitrary' a misnomer? Are not words &c parts & germinations of the Plant? And what is the Law of their Growth?—In

something of this order I would endeavour to destroy the old antithesis of *Words & Things,* elevating, as it were, words into Things, &
living Things too.

Here we have a foreshadowing or a hint of the distinction which Coleridge later made between the primary imagination which perceived the
external world and the secondary imagination which created new concepts, but here what is more important is the bringing of the two sorts of
conception together. When one remembers that "Things," the objects of
nature, were also for Coleridge here similar germinations of the creative
power, then one can see that he was now at the beginning of his attempt
to give the poet's word, and beyond that the Divine Word, the same
power and the same authority.

　The poem which embodied Coleridge's new ideas of nature and of joy
was first written in April 1802, as a letter to Sara Hutchinson, with
whom he had fallen in love, and it was based on the contrast between
Coleridge's miserable domestic life and that happiness and communion
with nature which Sara enjoyed as William Wordsworth's sister-in-law
and a member of his family group. It was not a situation which could be
described in a published poem, and so the verse letter was revised and
much shortened as "Dejection: an Ode," published in October of the
same year. The verse letter began with a description of Coleridge's
depressed state of mind, went on to a long description of his love for
Sara and his hopeless situation in his marriage, and rose to a conclusion
in the stanzas on the joy that Sara, as an innocent and loving being, was
able to feel, and on the One Life, here conceived as the joyful life within
us and its reflection in our perception of nature, that Sara should be able
to perceive. In the Ode, the fact that the poem had been addressed to
Sara Hutchinson was suppressed, all of the embarrassing personal matter was omitted, and the rest of the poem was rearranged so that most of
the material on the One Life is placed in the middle of the poem and
what remains of the detailed account of his misery follows it, with only a
short close returning to the One Life. Which is the better poem depends
on the reader's purposes. If one asks for elevation, decorum, and economy, then the Ode is undoubtedly better, and from that point of view
one can say with Griggs that Coleridge "turned a poetic letter full of self-
revelation and self-pity into a work of art with a timeless and universal
significance."[7] If one is interested in the human situation and the human
feelings revealed, then the letter is the better. But from a third point of
view, that of an interest in the ideas expressed, then the letter is again
the better because in it those ideas are set in, and illuminated by, their
context. Though the ideas of the poem were ones he had arrived at in

philosophy, they are here made part of his experience and we see them in action in his life.

The central concern of the poem is feeling and its power to shape the world about us. On this point the unity of the poem has sometimes been obscured by a misunderstanding of Coleridge's famous line, "My shaping spirit of Imagination." Here the word "Imagination" has often been given a sense drawn from the much later *Biographia Literaria* so as to make it a literary power (what Coleridge than called the secondary imagination) and thus to make the line a lament for Coleridge's loss of ability to write poetry; but here it is a power of perception that is in question, and the lament is for the loss of the power to perceive the life in nature. This point has been put succinctly by J. O. Hayden:

> Coleridge retains his capacity for expression, but not his 'shaping spirit of Imagination,' his capacity to get beyond mere detailed description. That the suspension is limited to joy and its attendant insight is a crucial point, for otherwise the wish in strophe VIII that the (non-poet) lady should have what he lacks would be absurd.[8]

With the loss of the imagination in this sense he has lost the power to shape the world into "fair forms and living motions."

In the letter this point is made through a contrast between Coleridge and Sara Hutchinson. Love is the precondition of joy (as it is in *The Ancient Mariner*) and the emphasis on Sara's loving and innocent nature is not just a compliment to her but an essential part of the contrast, just as Coleridge's description of his domestic unhappiness is not merely self-pity (though it may contain it), but an essential side of the contrast. His marriage, which ought to be his source of love and joy, has become a bitter conflict, poisoning even his love for his children and making his deep but innocent love for Sara Hutchinson herself something that can only bring her pain. When he comes to the passage on nature, it is this that sharpens the description:

> O Sara! we receive but what we give,
> And in *our* Life alone does Nature live.
> Our's is her Wedding Garment, our's her Shroud.—[9]

Life as wedding garment or as shroud sums the contrast. As House remarked,[10] it can be either.

In the letter (and, rather differently placed, in the Ode) there is mingled with the description of his misery what is the only important symbol in the poem, that of the Eolian harp. Introduced in the first stanza as dully sobbing in the wind that precedes the storm, and now heard after the "dark, distressful dream" of Sara's sickness and Coleridge's account of his personal unhappiness, it makes more violent music as the storm raves. It has a variety of music, but all tragic—"Thou Actor, perfect in all tragic sounds!"—and gives an image of Coleridge the poet making his music under the impulse of his turbulent and distressful feelings: as House says, "the possible wind-poems are thus possible Coleridge-poems."[11] The feelings which produce a perception of the world determine whether that perception will be of the "inanimate cold World" or whether it will be a vision which, in that symbol which had always represented joy to Coleridge, will be of that nature which is paradise, "A new Earth & a new Heaven." Similarly, just these feelings in the poet can produce the poems that embody either. Nevertheless, this is a subsidiary part of the contrast, and the main emphasis of the poem is on the power of love and joy to transform the world:

> Ah! from the Soul itself must issue forth
> A Light, a Glory, and a luminous Cloud
>   Enveloping the Earth!
> And from the Soul itself must there be sent
> A sweet and potent Voice, of it's own Birth,
> Of all sweet Sounds the Life & Element.[12]

His final address to Sara, the "Sister & Friend of my devoutest Choice," is as the "conjugal and mother Dove," at peace in the circle of those she loves and full of joy:

> Thus, thus should'st thou rejoice!
> To thee would all Things live from Pole to Pole,
> Their Life the Eddying of thy living Soul—[13]

Thus the "Letter" continues two of the main interests of Coleridge's early poetry—the discovery of the divine life in nature and the search for love and joy—but it does so in a new form that reflects the changing basis of Coleridge's faith. The divine life, the perception of which had earlier to be transmitted by God in nature to man, was now to be transmitted to nature by the divine creativity in man and that creativity was not a merely metaphysical power, alike for all men, but part of the individual's mental and spiritual makeup, affected by his spiritual state. Neither the joy nor the One Life in nature can be known "Save to the Pure and in their purest hour." This is the meaning of paradise, "A new Heaven & new Earth," and though the philosophical basis may be new, that is the point he had already made in *Kubla Khan* and *The Ancient Mariner*.

Coleridge thus needed to go on and explore this essentially psychological power that had now come to be central in his religious faith, and

Coleridge's powerful thirst for unity meant that, though the "Letter" was about perception, the final theory had to be much broader in its scope. The later developments of the theory of imagination are not particularly connected to ideas of symbolism, but the first developments of that theory did have very important consequences for romantic symbolism. Before the end of the year Coleridge had begun to make this distinction between "that inanimate cold World allow'd / To the poor loveless ever-anxious crowd" and the world of life created by joy and the shaping spirit of the imagination the basis for the first form of his distinction between imagination and fancy. In a letter of 10 September 1802 to Sotheby, Coleridge made his distinction in terms of the different ways of describing natural objects in Greek and Hebrew poetry respectively.

> The Greeks in their religious poems address always the Numina Loci, the Genii, the Dryads, the Naiads, &c &c—All natural Objects were *dead*—mere hollow Statues—but there was a Godkin or Godessling *included* in each—In the Hebrew Poetry you find nothing of this poor Stuff—as poor in genuine imagination, as it is mean in Intellect / —At best, it is but Fancy, or the aggregating Faculty of the mind—not *Imagination*, or the *modifying*, and *co-adunating* Faculty. This the Hebrew Poets appear to me to have possessed beyond all others—& next to them the English. In the Hebrew Poets each Thing has a Life of it's own, and they are all one Life.

The word "co-adunating" indicates that Coleridge was to some extent indebted to Kant's productive imagination, the *einbildungskraft*, and very possibly, for the concept of fancy, to Kant's associative imagination,[14] but this is not Kant's distinction nor his theory. This imagination is a psychological power that combines poetic vision with perception.

The theory of imagination has only an oblique bearing on symbolism, but its statement in this passage is important because, through its transmission by Wordsworth, it was the ultimate source of a new mythological symbolism in the work of the second generation of romantic poets. In view of his old interest in the Chaldean and Persian religions, it was probably Coleridge himself who developed this insight into what it became in Book 4 of Wordsworth's *Excursion*, that is, the idea that the religions and mythologies (for they were the same thing) of the Persians, Babylonians, and Chaldeans were intuitions and recognitions of the One Life in nature. Wordsworth dutifully attributed Greek mythology to the fancy, but he allowed imagination to some aspects of Greek religion, and in any case none of the second generation of romantic poets paid any attention to the now-celebrated distinction between imagination and fancy.

The ancient mythologies were thus both a way of perceiving nature and a representation of man's religious responses, a symbolism of both natural and emotional forces, and it was in this sense that Wordsworth's passages were taken up by the later poets[15] when *The Excursion* was published in 1814. The first of them to develop this hint into the symbolic myth that was the most distinctive form of the romantic long poem was Byron. The Persian engaged in worshiping nature on his mountain top appeared in the third canto (the "Wordsworthian" canto) of *Childe Harold's Pilgrimage:* a little later Peacock's suggestion, relayed by Shelley, that the Alpine glaciers were a fit dwelling for Ahriman, the *evil* spirit of the dualistic Persian religion, blended with Byron's reading of Goethe's *Faust* and of Aeschylus's *Prometheus Vinctus* to produce in his verse-drama *Manfred* a form that would symbolize both this pessimistic concept of nature and Byron's own "pageant of his bleeding heart," beginning with a chorus of nature spirits and moving on to a confrontation of the hero with Arimanes, the destructive "spirit of whatever is."

Shelley, who had also borrowed passages on the ancient religions from Wordsworth, used the form of *Manfred* and also of *Prometheus Vinctus* for his own more optimistic treatment of the nature of things in *Prometheus Unbound.* By taking his starting point in Aeschylus's myth, he based his poem directly on Greek mythology, but the world it represents is that of romantic nature and the One Life, and in it the forces of nature and man, and the spirits of nature and of human thought, evolve the action which finds its outcome in the perfection of both man and nature. Meanwhile, Keats had been moving independently in the same artistic direction. His favorite passage in Wordworth was the description of Greek mythology in *The Excursion* and he drew on it for his early poems, "I stood tiptoe" and the "first Endymion," and, as Leigh Hunt remarked at the time, for the theory of mythology which he embodied in them. From these he went on to the mythological-allegorical *Endymion* and eventually to a freer treatment of mythology in *Hyperion.* Thus there is a line to be traced from each of these poets back through *The Excursion* to Coleridge's original speculation.

It can be seen from all this that, in spite of the change in his philosophical justification of the idea, Coleridge was still concerned with the discovery of the divine in nature. Indeed, through the various changes in his thought there were certain religious concerns which remained constant (and others which dropped out), and this is the most persistent. Coleridge's career as a poet and as a thinker divides itself into three periods. The first began with his conversion to Unitarianism in 1794 and ended after his visit to Germany when he made the acquaintance of German idealist philosophy. This was the period when for him God was the essence of nature and when God, nature, and man were essentially spirit (Coleridge called himself "a naked spirit" in a letter to

Thelwall on 31 December 1796), and in this period nature was the symbolism or the language by which God communicated to man and the beauty of nature was the sign of his goodness. On the part of man the recognition of this divinity in nature required love and the mastery of the selfish passions, and in return it brought joy and illumination. The second period began with the study of Kant (and an acquaintance with Fichte) and lasted until the period he spent in Malta in 1804-6 and his conversion to Trinitarianism and the subsequent influence of Schelling. This second period, the time of the writing of the "Letter" and of the early development of his theory of imagination, was marked by what he called "Negative Unitarianism," a state in which he continued to dislike Trinitarianism and what he regarded as its immoral implications, but on the other hand abandoned Unitarian philosophy and theology. Instead he set about finding, through his new philosophical guides, fresh bases for the divinity which he felt in nature. Now instead of God, through nature, transmitting to man a sense of his divinity, in the new scheme the sense of the One Life was transmitted to nature from the divine power in man by the act of perception. The point in this which was unlike the theory of perception that Coleridge would have found in his new guides is that this act of perception involves the whole man and that again true perception involves love and purity. The third period was marked by Trinitarianism and the influence of Schelling, though there were variations in the strength of this last influence. This period was particularly marked by the employment of his new philosophical ideas in the defense of religion and by his sporadic attempts to adapt and develop theories of symbolism that would make clear the relationship between the highest reality and the appearances through which it can be known, and that would incidentally defend the rightness of the idea of a sacrament. The divine power in nature is still there (through the creative power in man) but its expression is a more intellectual thing than the joyful recognition of the earlier periods.

Still there also is the belief in a divinely inspired symbolism in the Scriptures, though this again takes a different form. In the 1790s Coleridge did not apply the term "symbol" to the prophetic language of Scripture, but from the beginning, following Priestley, he had combined some sort of quasi-literal belief in the millennium with the understanding that this represented a state of universal fraternal love. It was a state that God would bring about, but it was also God's metaphor for the joy and redemption which such love and such disciplining of the selfish passions can produce—a personal as well as a universal millennium. Effectively, God expressed himself in symbols in the Divine Word just as he did in nature. In this middle period the idea of biblical symbolism is less prominent, apart from the continuing identification of joy with the millennium, but there is a speculative suggestion that words themselves may be natural symbols, the natural outgrowths of perception. That speculation was dropped but the connection between perception and expression was explored further in the slowly developing theory of imagination. In its first form this dealt with the kind of perception that involved the emotions—indeed the whole man moral and emotional—and that produced that living world which is to be turned into the poetry that celebrates the One Life. With further refinement over the years, this power of perception was split into the primary imagination, which produces our primary perception of the world, that perception which is natural and common, and on the other hand the secondary imagination, which discovers qualities in what is perceived, reconciles oppositions, produces new concepts or figures, and serves the ends of poetry. This theory owes something to Schelling, particularly in the matter of the reconciliation of opposites, but it is something more psychological and less metaphysical than Schelling's power, and it is the end of a line of thought which began in this second period.

This theory of imagination did not concern itself with symbolism, but symbolism did regain some importance in Coleridge's last period, when he developed theories based on Kant's definition of a symbol and used these very effectively to explore the relations between suprasensuous ideas or laws in religion or politics and the sensuous embodiments or symbols through which they could be perceived and understood. This concept came to be of the first importance in a great deal of nineteenth-century thinking and was at least an important element in the influence which Coleridge exercised on many differing schools of thought.

What was lost in the last period was Coleridge's sense of joy. The poetry from 1795 to 1802 was centrally concerned with the quest for the love and joy that could be found in encounter with the divine. The sense of joy was always under threat from forces in which we may perhaps discern suggestions of the dark passions, or of unfeeling recklessness, or even of the ubiquitous evil of the world; and it was under threat too from Coleridge's feelings of guilt and worthlessness, however much he rejected such ideas. Nevertheless, the obverse to all this was the sense of being plucked from despair and being caught up into bliss and the family of love. Unfortunately, his later life was impoverished by laudanum and the withdrawal from it and by the deterioration of those relationships which had meant love to him. The sense of joy is still there as late as 1807 in his great poem "To William Wordsworth composed on the night after his recitation of a poem on the growth of an individual mind":

> Ah! as I listened with a heart forlorn,
> The pulses of my being beat anew:

And even as Life returns upon the drowned,
Life's joy rekindling roused a throng of pains—
Keen pangs of Love, awakening as a babe
Turbulent, with an outcry in the heart.[16]

But after the falling out with the Wordsworths and with Sara Hutchinson, which was Coleridge's banishment from the "family of Love," there are no more poems on joy and too many on the loss of hope. After this Coleridge's achievement was to be intellectual, not emotional, a tackling of the problems of belief rather than a celebration of encounter with the divine.

7

Symbolism and the Defense of Religion

THE year 1805, the year of Coleridge's stay in Malta, brought one very important change in Coleridge's religion, and that was his conversion to Trinitarianism. The change outlined in the last chapter, from a God communicating himself through the external world to a God communicating through the creative faculty in man, cut Coleridge off from those philosophers, from Hartley and Priestley to Berkeley and Spinoza, who had been the basis of his committed Unitarianism, but his dislike of Trinitarianism and what he regarded as its inevitable corollaries in doctrine remained very strong. He himself described his new position as negative Unitarianism and he clung to the unity of God and the optimistic view of God's purposes. He did not feel he could go further in positive doctrine than the beliefs of the Quakers, but he continued to describe Trinitarians as idolators. That, for him, this faith was as much moral in its force as it was philosophical is made clear in letters to other more positive Unitarians, as for instance in that to Coates on 5 December 1803:

> Believe me, I have never ceased to think of you with respect & a sort of yearning—you were the first man, from whom I heard that article of my Faith distinctly enunciated, which is the nearest to my Heart, the pure Fountain of all my moral & religious Feelings and Comforts—I mean, the absolute Impersonality of the Deity. The Many would deem me an Atheist; alas! I know them to be Idolaters.

But though there is still here the suggestion of strong moral repugnance to the doctrines of the Established Church, yet the new view of the nature of perception not only put the source of faith within man's mind but also by implication made the test of the truth of that faith not external argument but the way the faith fitted the nature of man's mind. A little more than a year after the letter to Coates, that is to say, on 12 February

1805, Coleridge reached a crisis of faith, which can be traced in his notebook. First comes a suggestion that the trinity *ad normam Platonis,* that is, as a philosophical description of the powers of man as Being, Intellect, and Spiritual Action could replace "the inanity of Jehovah, Christ, and the Dove," and this is followed by the realization that the idea will fit:

> The doctrines [of the Platonists] are strictly conformable with the true meaning of Plato and harmonizable with the doctrines of the orthodox Xstian.[1]

From this comes the religious conversion, carefully dated and timed at 1:30 P.M. of the same day (just as Pascal dated and timed his religious ecstasy) as an indication of its importance to him:

> It burst upon me at once as an awful Truth that 7 or 8 years ago I thought of proving. . . . No Christ, No God!—This I now feel with all its needful evidence . . .—that No Trinity, no God.—That Unitarianism in all its Forms is Idolatry.[2]

The line of thought is clear enough. If man is in God's image, then God and man must be congruent. A trinity in man and a simple unity in God are not really compatible, and the fact that the same trinity of powers fits both God and man is thus evidence of its truth. Equally clear is the wholehearted way in which Coleridge embraced his new faith and the scorn with which he now regarded those who were from henceforth cast in the role of "Idolaters."

Whatever the gains or losses represented by his new faith, Coleridge had now adopted an attitude of mind that could make his thinking considerably more flexible. Not very long after this, a note dated 14 April 1805 shows that Coleridge was making his first acquaintance with Schelling's view of nature, and that on a point which already concerned him, the relation between the external world and man's *moral* perceptions:

> In looking at objects of Nature while I am thinking, as at yonder moon dim-glimmering thro' the dewy window-pane, I seem rather to be seeking, as it were *asking,* a symbolical language for something within me that already and forever exists, than observing any thing new. Even when that latter is the case, yet still I have always an obscure feeling as if that new phaenomenon were the dim Awaking of a forgotten or hidden Truth of my inner Nature / It is still interesting as a Word, a Symbol! It is *Logos,* the Creator! and the Evolver![3]

Coleridge then went on to suggest that, though "another, foreign writer" had handled the same matter, these were ideas that he had "long meditated and perceived." The foreign writer who held these ideas must, of course, be Schelling, and Coleridge had not, in fact, shown anywhere that he had anticipated this particular point; but he had already adopted the general idea that the divine creative power in man gave both form and significance to the external world. What was new here was the idea that it does so by creating symbols with moral application. In these circumstances one might have expected that Coleridge would give himself to working out the implications of this view of symbolism, but that did not happen. Coleridge's further thoughts about symbolism were diffuse and unsystematic, only rising many years later to a more or less consistently worked-out theory of his own.

The main studies of Coleridge as a philosopher, from Muirhead to McFarland,[4] have been concerned with the major issues of his thought and so have rightly given little attention to his entanglements with symbolism. Indeed Coleridge's later views or borrowings on the subject of symbolism were certainly not as numerous nor as concordant as one would wish. As Patricia Ward says, they comprise "a few brilliant statements which adapt in a meaningful way the symbol as seen by Schelling or Schlegel to the Englishman's own aesthetic theories, but Coleridge the theorist never became the spokesman for the symbol to the degree with which the Germans were its enthusiasts."[5] There is perhaps a little more to it than this, but it is true to say that it is not easy to untangle his theories of symbolism in this period as they appear in his writings: the great difficulty in giving an account of them is that he did not hold any one consistent theory, so that his statements cannot be put together into a single system. He often used the word "symbol" in quite ordinary accepted senses without any suggestion of theory: at other times he paraphrased or took theories from Goethe, A. W. Schlegel, or Schelling, and at other times again he produced his own variations on these. Finally, when he did produce a set of ideas that caught up his lifelong interests and that was firmly his own, he was quite capable of explaining his definition in a way that was quite at variance with the original thought and that plunged the whole matter into confusion (and suspicion) again.

To illustrate the problem of trying to deal coherently with the ideas of symbolism contained in Coleridge's later writings, it is worthwhile listing some of the miscellaneous uses he made of the term. Thus at different times he spoke of the trees planted in Hamburg as "the pledges and symbols of a long peace," of the evaporation of water as "a symbol of taxation," of "the acts and objects of a tradesman's craft" as "the symbols of all doctrines and duties" for him, of the falsity of thinking of the Logos as "a mere personification or symbol," of "the earth with its scarred face as a symbol of the past: the air and the heaven of futurity," and once quite indifferently of "symbols and emblems."[6]

Nevertheless, even if he was not at all consistent in his use of the word, Coleridge did have a number of ideas about symbolism and, as he sometimes seemed to have more than one theory in play in a given period, it is best to deal with these theories separately and not chronologically. The general background to his thinking was Kantian and post-Kantian German philosophy, particularly that of Kant, Schlegel, and Schelling. In Kant's definition, which lies behind all of these theories, a symbol was the sensuous representation of a suprasensuous reality, that is, of a kind of entity which is real but is not accessible to the senses.[7] An example, though an example of only one kind of such an entity, might be a scientific law, and the symbols might then be the facts or phenomena to which it gives rise, while the law could be contemplated in a different aspect as an idea, not unlike a Platonic form. Coleridge adopted this point of view in *The Friend,* where he wrote:

> As little can a true scientific method be grounded on an hypothesis, unless where the hypothesis is an exponential of image or picture-language of an *idea* which is contained in it more or less clearly; or the symbol of an undiscovered law.[8]

A little further on he wrote:

> Bacon. . .names the laws of nature, *ideas;* and represents what we have. . .called *facts of science* and *central phenomena,* as signatures, impressions, and symbols of ideas.[9]

In the same way he wrote that the "indecomponible substances of the LABORATORY are the symbols of chemical powers."[10]

The ideas or laws were not only laws of natural science. Coleridge wrote that the belief in a spiritual God was excited in the patriarchs as idea and, since they were forbidden images, communicated by symbols which were "as far as possible, *intellectual.*"[11] The whole theory had important theological implications for Coleridge. Kant had written in the *Critique of Judgement* that "all our knowledge of God is symbolic," and that "a person who regards it as schematic" (as opposed by symbolic) "falls into anthropomorphism."[12] To translate this into simpler, if less philosophical, language, if we regard our knowledge of God as plainly descriptive, then our notion of God will be anthropomorphic and wrong: on the other hand, the ways in which we know God are not simply figurative; they are the sensuous means by which we know a suprasensuous reality and they bear the kind of relation to the truth of

God that natural phenomena bear to the scientific truths they express. In this context a symbol is not a matter of arbitrary choice but the natural expression of the idea which it represents.

In dealing with theological matters the advantage for Coleridge of Kant's theory is obvious: it preserves the absoluteness of the suprasensuous reality while making its sensuous representation in symbol not a mere simile but the natural and proper way of apprehending the reality concerned. This is the point of a passage in *On the Constitution of Church and State:*

> The mistaking of symbols and analogies for metaphors . . . has been a main occasion and support of the worst errors in Protestantism; so the understanding the same symbols in a literal *i.e. phaenomenal* sense, notwithstanding the most earnest warnings against it, the most express declarations of the folly and danger of interpreting *sensually* what was delivered of objects *super*sensual [is the mark of papal superstition].[13]

This gave Coleridge his defense of the sacramental nature of the Lord's Supper, which he defended in *The Statesman's Manual* in a shift away from his old abhorrence of it (though he still did not take that sacrament again until a visit to Cambridge in 1827). It also provided him with an approach to the Scriptures (and particularly to the Old Testament, which he treated not as historical evidences but as symbolic accounts of divine dealing with man).

This application of the theory of symbolism to the mode of religious belief, as well as to the laws and phenomena of natural science, seems to have set Coleridge dreaming in the 1820s of a philosophy which would embrace both. On 20 January 1820 he wrote to C. A. Tulk:

> If I mistake not one philosophical formula would comprize your philosophical faith and mine—namely that the sensible world is but an evolution of Truth, Love and Life, or their opposites, in Men—and that in Nature man beholds only (to use an algabraic but close analogy) the integration of the Products, the Differentials of which are in, and constitute, his own mind and soul—and consequently that all true science is contained in the Lore of Symbols and Correspondences.

This talk of the evolution of moral ideas shows the influence of Schelling, but the doctrine of symbolism was common to Kant and his successors, and subsequent letters show that he had in mind Kant's doctrine of our symbolic knowledge of God. On 26 January 1824 he wrote again to Tulk of the symbolic sense of the Scriptures, where the literal sense is body and the symbolic sense is soul; and on 13 February

1824 he wrote that "all real science is mythological," and that the cosmos is a most sacred myth. Finally on 8 September 1826 he wrote to Tulk

> of the connection obetween Symbols & Correspondences of the written Word (i.e. the Scriptures) and those of the visible Creation—and whether a certain Philosophy of Symbols might not unite all the Friends of a spiritual faith, so as they might co-operate so far.

But Coleridge, despite an intermittent interest in chemistry, was a very long way from being a natural scientist, and the project lapsed, as it must have. Nevertheless, in the fields of politics and religion, his transmission of the theory of ideas and their symbols was of the greatest influence and importance.

The other major source of ideas on symbolism for Coleridge, mingling with the Kantian ideas just described, was the philosophy of Schelling. This philosophy, translated or paraphrased, constituted a large part of *Biographia Literaria*, as well as almost, but not quite, the whole of the essay "On Poesy or Art." In *Biographia Literaria* the word occurs only a few times, and then only in neutral senses, except on one occasion, in a passage drawn from Schelling where Coleridge wrote:

> An IDEA, in the *highest* sense of that word, cannot be conveyed but by a *symbol*; and, except in geometry, all symbols of necessity involve an apparent contradiction.[14]

Both the words "idea" and "symbol" and the notion of contradiction here have the special senses they assume in Schelling's philosophy, forming part of his system. What Schelling brought to German idealist philosophy was that he saw the universe as a process in which intelligence both creates and is conscious of creating, and this creation involves the reconciliation of opposites. In particular the imagination is the power which advances this process, and creates the world we know, by reconciling the two fundamental opposites of subjective and objective. (Schelling remarked the imagination was "the only faculty in which we are able to think and understand even the contradictory.")[15] The appearances of nature, thus grasped by the imagination and embodying the perceiving intelligence, were thus symbols, and, because they did have intelligence in them, they exhibited that One Life, without us and within, that had always been so important to Coleridge. What underlay the whole process was that what was at the base of perceived nature was the spirit or soul, which, for Schelling, unlike Coleridge, was "not the principle of individuality."[16] It was spirit in this impersonal sense that Schelling meant when he said that "Nature is visible Spirit, Spirit is invisible Nature."[17]

This is the philosophy to be found in Schelling's *Academy Oration* of 1806,[18] which Coleridge largely paraphrased in his lecture "On Poesy or Art." Both Schelling's theory and Coleridge's small but important divergence from it can be illustrated by quotation from Coleridge's lecture. (The order of the extracts has been slightly altered so as to make the exposition clearer.) At the beginning here Coleridge followed Schelling very closely:

> Nature itself would give us the impression of a work of art, if we could see the thought which is present at once in the whole and in every part. . . . The artist must imitate that which is within the thing, that which is active through form and figure, and discourses to us by symbols—the *Natur-geist* or spirit of nature. . . . Man's mind is the very focus of all the rays of intellect which are scattered throughout the images of nature. Now so to. . .elicit from, and to superinduce upon, the forms themselves the moral reflexions to which they approximate, to make the external internal, the internal external, to make nature thought, and thought nature,—this is the mystery of genius in the Fine Arts. . . . [The artist must acquire] living and life-producing ideas, which shall contain their own evidence, the certainty that they are essentially one with the germinal causes in nature,—his consciousness being the focus and mirror of both.[19]

Here Coleridge adds a sentence that is not in Schelling and is not Schelling's theory nor his emphasis, but Coleridge's own:

> For of all we see, hear, feel and touch the substance is and must be in ourselves; and therefore there is no alternative in reason between the dreary (and, thank heaven! almost impossible) belief that every thing around us is but a phantom, or that the life which is in us is in them likewise.[20]

For Schelling the common substance was the impersonal intellect, soul or spirit (*geist*). In speaking of "the life which is in us" Coleridge was harking back to the "Letter to Asra" and his own psychological explanation of the perception of that life. As Herbert Read says of the lecture generally, "where Schelling speaks of impersonal forces and abstract forms, Coleridge everywhere inserts the human element."[21]

When Coleridge wrote the "Letter to Asra" he had not yet read Schelling. We can see how this common thread of living nature might lead Coleridge to the belief that he had anticipated Schelling, and even to the claim that he had done so before Schelling's earliest important publications, for this belief in the life in nature goes back to Coleridge's early manhood. Nevertheless, this faith was not in any way a *philosophical* anticipation, and the common thread is no more, at base, than

Schelling's and Coleridge's common "pantheism." Poems describing the presence of God in nature and explaining it in different ways are common, particularly in the eighteenth century; but, though they represent religious positions, they are not necessarily philosophical statements,[22] and Coleridge's early poetry does not contain any hint of Schelling's philosophical position.

Nevertheless, Coleridge had now found in Schelling a new basis for his lifelong belief in the divinity of nature, reconciled here with the divinity in man's own soul, and in *The Statesman's Manual* he applied it most fully to both natural and biblical symbolism. One theme that had run continuously through Coleridge's thought on natural symbolism had been the ultimate identity of the outward manifestation—the symbol—with the inner essence or reality, whether that be the divine life in nature, which, as early as 1796, he had called nature's essence, or the One Life that is the effect of the creative power in man, which is an image in him of the Creator. This line of thought casts light on what critics have often found a puzzling passage in Coleridge's definition of a symbol in; *The Statesman's Manual*, where he says that a symbol always partakes of (and is consubstantial with) the reality which it represents.[23] This reality, both in nature and in Scripture, is, of course, God, whose word they both are; it is because God is the essence of nature and the truth in the Scriptures that the appearances of both partake of him. Applying this more widely is a different matter, although J. A. Hodgson, in the course of a good discussion of the allegory-symbol distinction, offers the possible but rather desperate suggestion that "all synecdoches would seem indifferently valid symbols of the universal Presence."[24] Really there is no way in which this can apply to ordinary literary symbolism: when Coleridge himself later tried to make it apply to figurative language generally, the result was absurd.

> *A symbol is a sign included in the idea it represents: ex.gr.* an actual *part* chosen to represent the *whole*, as a lip with the chin prominent is a Symbol of Man.[25]

Equally disastrous was the example he gave elsewhere of a sail as the symbol of a ship.[26] The same problem occurs in J. R. Barth's *The Symbolic Imagination*, where an excellent treatment of natural symbolism is followed by an attempt to apply the same principles to Yeats and Eliot:[27] the staircases and the tarot pack are symbols, but they do not seem to be in a sacramental relationship with God.

In *The Statesman's Manual*, as M. H. Abrams has pointed out,[28] Coleridge was concerned with only two kinds of symbolism, biblical and natural—the symbolism of the book of the Scriptures and that of the book of nature, which is much narrower than the range which he had given to imagination in the *Biographia Literaria*. Indeed there is a considerable shift of position: as Kathleen Wheeler says, the *Biographia* is the only one of Coleridge's works to stress the primacy of imagination, and she suggests, following Thomas McFarland, that he retreated on this point because of its implications of pantheism.[29] In works written later, including *The Statesman's Manual*, imagination becomes the mediator between reason and the images of sense, so that, though imagination retains its function of giving sensuous expression to suprasensuous ideas, it now does so in the service of the transcendental reason, the power to grasp principles: indeed, in discussing the symbolism of Holy Writ it would be unsatisfactory to have it otherwise.

Before discussing the application of this theory to Scripture, it is helpful to look at his treatment of the other book of God, the book of nature. Though his account retains features of *Naturphilosophie*, his emphasis is not on *Natur-geist*, Schelling's spirit of Nature, but on nature as the thought of God:

> The human mind is the compass, in which the laws and actuations of all outward essences are revealed. . . . It is a problem of which God is the only solution, God, the one before all, and of all, and through all!—True natural philosophy is comprized in the study of the science and language of *symbols*. The power delegated to nature is all in every part: and by a symbol I mean, not a metaphor or allegory or any other figure of speech or form of fancy, but an actual and essential part of that, the whole of which it represents.[30]

Thus the symbols embody the power delegated by God to nature and so are parts of that power which they represent. Nevertheless, the enterprise of understanding the world through this symbolism was doomed to failure. To attempt to intuit from the appearances of nature not only the laws of nature but also the powers of God, as well as a series of "moral reflections to which they approximate" (sought in later works as well as here)—all embodied in the symbolism while keeping the whole thing within the domain of natural science—now seems simply misguided. *Naturphilosophie* was a dead end in the history of thought, and one might well prefer Coleridge's earlier, but less dated, Platonic intuition that love of the beauty of the world leads to love of God.

The application of his ideas to the Bible was a different matter and much more his own. Coleridge had long been a believer in the inspiration of the Scriptures, as opposed to the literal interpretation of them. He was not so much concerned with the literal truth as he was with their spiritual and theological truth: for instance, he was willing, on one occasion, to doubt the truth of the description of the Ascension,[31] a surprising example of criticism in a believer of that period. (He did believe in the general physical truth of the biblical narrations, but it coexisted with the symbolic truth.) Here again he approached the problem through his theory of symbolism, but it must be realized that the biblical symbols he speaks of are not figures of speech but persons and their actions, the transactions of God with man. As symbols these embody truths grasped by the transcendental reason:

> In the Scriptures they are the living *educts* of the Imagination; of that reconciling and mediatory power, which incorporating the Reason in Images of the Sense, and organizing (as it were) the flux of the Senses by the permanence and self-circling energies of the Reason, gives birth to a system of symbols, harmonious in themselves, and consubstantial with the truths, of which they are the *conductors*.[32]

It is easy to see that a natural symbol is part of nature. It is less easy to see how the words which constitute a biblical system should be consubstantial with the truths until one remembers that these are not secular stories but part of "the Sacred Book. . . worthily intitled *the* WORD OF GOD." To illustrate this, Coleridge turned to Ezekiel's chariot, which contained the spirit of God even in its wheels:

> These are the Wheels which Ezekiel beheld, when the hand of the Lord was upon him. . . . *Whithersoever the Spirit was to go, the wheels went, and thither was their spirit to go, for the spirit of the living creature was in the wheels also*. The truths and the symbols that represent them move in conjunction and form the living chariot that bears up (for *us*) the throne of the Divine Humanity.[33]

Hence a symbol, biblical or natural, "always partakes of that Reality which it renders intelligible."[34]

What this way of thinking does is to turn aside the new (largely, at this date, German) criticism of the Bible. Coleridge, as a Unitarian, was early aware of this criticism, as is evidenced by his reading of the German historical critic Michaelis and his interest in German scepticism.[35] In any case, the man who objected on moral grounds to the doctrine of the atonement was not likely to be much taken by a theory of literal truth: a text like "Happy shall he be that taketh and dasheth thy little ones against the stones"[36] could disturb even the most traditional reader. Indeed Coleridge wrote in *Aids to Reflection*:

> [The Bible is] so strangely written, that in a series of the most concerning points including. . .all the *peculiar* Tenets of the Religion, the plain and obvious meaning of the words . . . is no sufficient guide to their actual sense or to the Writer's own Meaning![37]

A modern approach to Scripture might stress the primitiveness of its early documents and the primitive nature of the religious insights embodied in them. Coleridge instead avoids the problems by stressing the symbolic nature of the understanding expressed, thus preserving both the authority of the Bible and the moral nature of the Old Testament God. These symbols can be trusted because the spirit of God is in them and it is through them that we can reach the suprasensuous reality that is otherwise beyond us. On this theory, then, it can be seen that understanding the Bible is not unlike understanding poetry: in each we reach through the imaginative embodiment to the truth beyond. Something of this was behind Matthew Arnold when he insisted that the essence of religion was poetry and not fact—except that Coleridge does not abandon the fact, and for him, the imaginative poetry is a way of understanding God and not an end in itself.

Coleridge's application of this doctrine of symbolism thus covered the discovery of God in nature, the word of God in the Scriptures, and the divine nature of the sacraments, but it also went beyond this, covering natural laws and their phenomena and finally those cases of idea and embodiment exemplified by political and social institutions. The influence of transcendental philosophy would have, and did, come in eventually from other sources; but Coleridge was first, he was sensitive to what had to be explained, and his influence is very widely diffused in English nineteenth-century thought. But if his later work was important in apologetics—the art of reconciling faith with the current climate of opinion in a particular age—yet his earlier work, and particularly his best poetry, was concerned not with apologetics but with religious experience. Coleridge was always a religious man. On 3 February 1804 Coleridge wrote to Godwin to apologize for a vehement and rather drunken defense of his faith but, though he expressed regrets, Coleridge nevertheless did not yield on the main point:

> I have at all times, (most unbelievable by those who only know the two or three first *Coatings* of my Being) a most intense Faith in my religious opinions, such as they are. . . . I felt & thought, as if the meanest man having such a Faith, & living under it as his ultimate Principle of action, was as a God, compared with the most illustrious of those who have disciplined their minds & hearts in disbelief.

As his phrase "such as they are" suggests, Coleridge's religious opinions were of great simplicity. The important points were the presence of the divine in the world, the illumination that encounter with God brings, the discipline and love that conquer the dark passions and bring universal fraternal love, the family of love that is the kingdom of heaven, and the joy that is its reward. But if the faith was intellectually simple (no bad thing for one who seeks to enter the kingdom of heaven), yet it was, in its expression in the poetry, emotionally very rich. This expression is largely personal. Coleridge did, in his younger days at any rate, share the other side of the biblical prophets—their yearning for justice, their hatred of the oppression of man by man and of the grinding of the faces of the poor—but the expression of these things was not symbolical, and poetically they fell on barren ground to be the easy prey of lampoonists. On the other hand the great poems have an emotional complexity that comes from the action and interaction of ancient symbols with complicated histories.

At the same time it should be noticed that, though the symbolism of the Conversation Poems has been deepened emotionally beyond that of their eighteenth-century predecessors, yet the poems remain overtly religious poems, dealing with the encounter with the divine. On the other hand the three great poems of the year 1797–98 are detached, in their subject matter, from religious concerns. They are about a khan and a poet-prophet, a mariner with a curse on him, and a meeting with a strange being from the eldritch world. The way in which religion enters is that Coleridge thought about their concerns in religious ways and in religious categories, using historic forms of religious symbolism that could not but help but bring with them religious insights. The fact that the themes themselves had been secularized was important because the influence of these poems was then secular and they gave their richness of symbolic freedom to poems about ordinary concerns and ordinary feelings. Either through Wordsworth or directly, Coleridge's gift of a free emotional symbolism reached Byron, Shelley, and Keats; directly and with particular emphasis on its emotional quality, it reached Poe and through him Baudelaire and the Symbolists. Coleridge's place in the progress of poetry is perhaps nowhere more fascinatingly seen than in relation to the line that runs through him from Ezekiel to Yeats.

Notes

Full bibliographical details of works (other than those by S. T. Coleridge) cited will be found in Works Cited. For works by S. T. Coleridge, the abbreviations used are:

AR   S. T. Coleridge. *Aids to Reflection*. London: 1831.

BL   S. T. Coleridge. *Biographia Literaria and his aesthetical essays*. Edited by J. Shawcross. Oxford: Clarendon Press, 1907.

CC   *The Collected Works of Samuel Taylor Coleridge*. Edited by K. Coburn. Princeton: Princeton University Press, 1969–.

CL   *The Collected Letters of Samuel Taylor Coleridge*. Edited by E. L. Griggs. Oxford: Clarendon Press, 1956–71.

MAL *Miscellanies, Aesthetic and Literary. . . .* London: G. Bell, 1885.

MC   *Coleridge's Miscellaneous Criticism*. Edited by T. M. Raysor. London: Constable, 1936.

NB   *The Notebooks of Samuel Taylor Coleridge*. Edited by K. Coburn. New York: Pantheon, 1957–.

PL   S. T. Coleridge. *Philosophical Lectures (1819)*. Edited by K. Coburn. London: Pilot, 1949.

PW   *The Poems of Samuel Taylor Coleridge*. Edited by E. H. Coleridge. Oxford: Clarendon Press, 1912. Quotations are from this edition.

TT   *Table Talk and Omniana of Samuel Taylor Coleridge*. Edited by T. Ashe. London: George Bell, 1888.

Preface

1. *CL*, 1:625.
2. *CL*, 2:1193.
3. Ibid.

Chapter 1. Symbolism and Coleridge's Religion

1. W. B. Yeats, *Selected Prose*, ed. A. N. Jeffares (London: Macmillan, 1964), 235.

2. S. Potter, *Coleridge and STC* (London: Jonathan Cape, 1935), 232; D. G. James, *The Romantic Comedy* (London: Oxford University Press, 1948), 197; A. S. Gerard, *English Romantic Poetry* (Berkeley and Los Angeles: University of California Press, 1968), 42; R. L. Brett, "Coleridge's Theory of Imagination," *Essays and Studies*, n.s. 2 (1949): 78.

3. *CL*, 2:820–22, 1022–23. For the continuity of Coleridge's views on original sin, redemption, regeneration, grace, and justification, see *The Destiny of Nations* 85; "The Eolian Harp 61; *Religious Musings* 88, 92, 75–78.

4. J. R. Barth, *Coleridge and Christian Doctrine* (Cambridge: Harvard University Press, 1969), 141–42.

5. The account of Unitarianism that follows is based on the following: T. Belsham, *Memoirs of the Reverend Theophilus Lindsey* (London, 1812); O. M. Griffiths, *Religion and Learning* (Cambridge: Cambridge University Press, 1935); R. V. Holt, *The Unitarian Contribution to Social Progress in England*, 2nd ed. (London: Lindsey, 1952); H. McLachlan, *The Unitarian Movement in the Religious Life of England* (London: Allen and Unwin, 1934); *The Dictionary of National Biography* s. vv. "William Frend," "Joseph Priestley."

6. B. Willey, *The Eighteenth Century Background* (London: Chatto and Windus, 1946), 168–204.

7. Griffiths, *Religion and Learning*, 22–23; Holt, *The Unitarian Contribution to Social Progress*, 25.

8. B. Willey, *Samuel Taylor Coleridge* (London: Chatto and Windus, 1972), 80, 87.

9. McLachlan, *The Unitarian Movement in the Religious Life of England*, 13.

10. H. McLachlan, *The Religious Opinions of Milton, Newton and Locke* (Manchester: Manchester University Press, 1941), 17–18, 146ff.

11. Griffiths, *Religion and Learning*, 153.

12. McLachlan, *The Unitarian Movement in the Religious Life of England*, 26–27, 13–67 passim; Belsham *Memoirs of Theophilus Lindsey*, 215–16, 236–37; and cf. *CL*, 5:611.

13. Griffiths, *Religion and Learning*, 126.

14. *Religious Musings* 395 note.

15. *Religious Musings* 367–68.

16. J. Priestley *The Conclusion of Dr Hartley's Observations* (London, 1794); Priestley, *The Present State of Europe compared with Antient Prophecies* (London, 1794).

17. *NB*, N83.

18. *CC*, 1:lxxiv, lxxv, 13; *Religious Musings* 148–58, 341.

19. *CL*, 1:103.

20. *CL*, 2:1022–23.

21. E. K. Chambers, *Samuel Taylor Coleridge* (Oxford: Clarendon Press, 1938), 57.

22. *NB*, N2448.

23. T. De Quincey, *Works*, ed. D. Masson (Edinburgh: P. and C. Black, 1889), 2:144; *The Letters of Charles and Mary Lamb*, ed. E. W. Marrs (Ithaca: Cornell University Press, 1975), 1:183; W. Hazlitt, *Works*, ed. P. P. Howe (London: Dent, 1930–34), 7:183. See also Wordsworth's opinion quoted in chapter 5 below.

24. *NB*, N2546.

25. *BL*, 1:102, 114.

26. *BL*, 1:102, 114; and, e.g., E. R. Wasserman, "The English Romantics: The Grounds of Knowledge," *Studies in Romanticism*, 4 (1964): 29–31; L. J. Forstner, "Coleridge's 'The Ancient Mariner' and the case for justifiable mythocide," *Criticism* 18 (1976): 225; K. M. Wheeler, *The Creative Mind in Coleridge's Poetry* (London: Heinemann, 1981), 7–10.

27. Wheeler, *The Creative Mind in Coleridge's Poetry*, 160.

28. R. Wellek, *A History of Modern Criticism, 1750–1950*, (New Haven: Yale University Press, 1953), 2:156–57; G. N. G. Orsini, *Coleridge and German Idealism* (Carbondale: Southern Illinois University Press, 1969), 217ff.; N. Fruman, *Coleridge the Damaged Archangel* (New York: G. Braziller, 1972), 85–91.

29. *NB*, N2447.

30. *Religious Musings* 1–23 app. crit.; *CC*, 1:200.

31. *AR*, 147–48. He adopted Calvinism when he became Trinitarian; see Chambers, *Samuel Taylor Coleridge*, 204.

32. *AR*, 152–53, 301ff.

33. *Religious Musings* 185.

34. Hazlitt, *Works*, 17:113.

35. *CC*, 10:106.

36. W. Empson and D. Pirie, eds., *Coleridge's Verse: A Selection* (London: Faber, 1972), 99.

37. G. W. Hegel, *Saemtliche Werke* (Stuttgart: Fromann, 1956–59), 15:110.

38. *BL*, 2:112–13.

39. *CL*, 1:192–93. For another common misunderstanding, see H. W. Piper, "Coleridge's Note on Unitarianism, Orthodoxy and Atheism," *Notes and Queries*, n.s. 25 (1978): 220–21.

40. *CL*, 1:372.

41. *Religious Musings* 49.

42. J. Priestley, *Matter and Spirit* (London, 1777), 235–36.

43. H. W. Frei, *The Eclipse of Biblical Narrative* (New Haven: Yale University Press, 1974), *passim*.

44. M. Jacobus, "William Huntington's 'Spiritual Sea-voyage': another source for 'The Ancient Mariner,'" *Notes and Queries*, n.s. 16 (1969): 409–12.

45. T. Hobbes, *Leviathan*, ed. J. S. Thornton (Oxford: Clarendon Press, 1881), 360.

46. *Religious Musings* 395–401; *Ode to the Departing Year* 141–44 and note.

Chapter 2. Natural Symbolism and the Conversation Poems

1. *CC*, 1:204 note.

2. *TT*, 23 June 1834.

3. *Religious Musings* 359 note.

4. *CC*, 1:216 note.

5. H. W. Piper, *The Active Universe* (London: Athlone, 1962), 33, 38.

6. *Dictionary of National Biography*, s.v. "William Frend."

7. *CC*, 1:94; M. Akenside, *The Pleasures of Imagination* (second version), in *Poetical Works*, ed. Gilfillan (Edinburgh: James Nichol, 1857), 1:99–108, 3:279–86, 625–33.

8. *CC* 1:158; E. Young, *Night Thoughts*, ed. Gilfillan (Edinburgh: James Nichol, 1853), Night Nine 1659–63; and see *OED* s.v. "Symbol," sense 3.

9. *The Destiny of Nations* 18–20.

10. J. Priestley, *Theological and Miscellaneous Works*, ed. J. T. Rutt (London, 1817), 2:465, 451.

11. *Religious Musings* 1–23 app. crit.

12. *Religious Musings* 14–16.

13. W. K. Wimsatt, *The Verbal Icon* (New York: Noonday, 1958), 108–9; A. Matheson, "The Influence of Cowper's 'The Task' on Coleridge's Conversation Poems," in *New Approaches to Coleridge*, ed. D. S. Sultana, (1981), 142.

14. *NB*, N556.

15. W. J. Bate, *Coleridge* (New York: Macmillan, 1968), 33.

16. *Religious Musings* 127–31.

17. "The Eolian Harp" (second draft) 36–46.

18. "The Eolian Harp" 44–48.

19. See K. Everest, *Coleridge's Secret Ministry: The Context of the Conversation Poems of 1795–8* (Hassocks: Harvester, 1979), 203–21; see also *CL*, 1:278.

20. E.g., C. G. Martin, "Coleridge and Cudworth: A Source for 'The Eolian Harp,'" *Notes and Queries*, n.s. 13 (1966): 173; Wheeler, *The Creative Mind in Coleridge's Poetry*, 81; D. Jaspers, *Coleridge as Poet and Religious Thinker* (London: Macmillan, 1985), 36.

21. *PL*, 371.

22. *BL*, 1:81.

23. "Reflections on having left a place of retirement" 29–37.

24. "Lines: composed while climbing the Left Ascent of Brockley Coomb, Somersetshire, May 1795" 12–16.

25. "Reflections on having left a place of retirement" 38–42.

26. *Religious Musings* 37–45.

27. *The Destiny of Nations* 253–75.

28. Genesis 15:12.

29. D. V. Erdman, "Unrecorded Coleridge Variants," *Studies in Bibliography* 11 (1958): 151–53.

30. M. Moorman, *Wordsworth, a Biography: The Early Years, 1770–1803* (London: Oxford University Press, 1957), 25–40.

31. "Lines Left upon a Seat in a Yew-Tree" 48–49.

32. G. Marcel, *Coleridge et Schelling* (Paris: Aubier Montaigne, 1971), 36.

33. *PW*, 102.

34. W. Schrickx, "Coleridge and the Cambridge Platonists," *Review of English Literature* 7 (1966): 81.

35. "This Lime-tree Bower" 10–19.

36. "Frost at Midnight" 54–62.

37. *CL*, 1:406.

38. F. V. Randell, "Coleridge and the Contentiousness of Romantic Nightingales," *Studies in Romanticism* 21 (1982): 35ff.

39. "The Nightingale" 77–86.

40. Euripides, *Bacchae* 185.

41. "Ode to a Nightingale" 23–24.

42. "The Nightingale" 14–15.

Chapter 3. Biblical, Natural, and Gothic Symbolism in *The Ancient Mariner*

1. E.g., M. H. Abrams, *Natural Supernaturalism* (New York: W. W. Norton, 1971); H. W. Piper, *Nature and the Supernatural in "The Ancient Mariner"* (Armidale: University of New England, 1956); idem, *The Active Universe*.

2. R. Garnham, *A Sermon preached in the Chapel of Trinity College, Cambridge . . . December 19, 1793* (Cambridge, 1794); *The British Critic* 7 (October 1796): 430; J. Priestley, *The Present State of Europe compared with Antient Prophecies* (London, 1794); idem, *Conclusion to Hartley's Observations;* I. Newton, *Opera*, ed. S. Horsley (London, 1779–85), 5:305–9; *NB*, N83.

3. *Religious Musings* 317–22, 309–13, 332; *The Destiny of Nations* 448–50.

4. *The Destiny of Nations* 437–39.

5. Newton, *Opera*, 5:305–9; NB, N83; *The Destiny of Nations* 421 app. crit., 429 app. crit.; *Ode to the Departing Year* 33–37 app. crit.

6. 1 Corinthians 15:23–24.

7. *NB*, N174(7).

8. *NB*, N133; *Religious Musings* 359 app. crit.

9. *PW*, 112.

10. *The Ancient Mariner* 446–51.

11. *Religious Musings* 346–54.

12. *Religious Musings* 153–58.

13. *Religious Musings* 359 note.

14. *CL*, 1:396.

15. *PW*, 495.

16. J. B. Beer, "Coleridge and Boehme's 'Aurora,'" *Notes and Queries* n.s. 10 (1963):183–87.

17. *NB*, N273.

18. "Reflections on having left a place of retirement" 37–38.

19. W. H. Auden, *The Enchafed Flood* (London: Faber, 1951), 23.

20. S. Purchas, *Hakluytus Posthumus; or Purchas his Pilgrimes* (London, 1625), 1:6.
21. Moorman, *William Wordsworth, The Early Years*, 348.
22. *BL*, 2:120.
23. T. Burnet, *The Sacred Theory of the Earth*, 2 ed. (London, 1691), 2:78.
24. Piper, *The Active Universe*, 93–96.
25. *The Ancient Mariner* 123–30.
26. *The Ancient Mariner* 269–71.
27. Piper, "Shakespeare's 'Antony and Cleopatra' V ii 279–81," *The Explicator* 26 (1967): 10.
28. *The Ancient Mariner* 236–39.
29. Newton, *Opera*, 5:307.
30. *Religious Musings* 346–54.
31. E. Darwin, *The Botanic Garden* (London, 1791), 1. 4. 307–20 note; *NB*, N133.
32. *Religious Musings* 359–61 app. crit.
33. *The Ancient Mariner* 454–55.
34. The Ancient Mariner 358–70.
35. *The Ancient Mariner* 341–44.
36. Empson and Pirie, *Coleridge's Verse: a Selection, 99.*
37. *The Ancient Mariner* 546–55.
38. *The Ancient Mariner* 582–55.
39. *The Ancient Mariner* 596–600.
40. *The Ancient Mariner* 616–17.
41. D. H. Lawrence, *Apocalypse* (London: Martin Secker, 1932), 77.
42. "Resolution and Independence" 130–31.

Chapter 4. Paradisal Symbolism in *Kubla Khan*

1. E. W. Schneider, *Coleridge, Opium and "Kubla Khan"* (Chicago: University of Chicago Press, 1966), 169.
2. Moorman, *William Wordsworth, The Early Years*, 412–13.
3. *PW*, 296.
4. M. Robinson, *Poems* (London, 1803) 1:226–28.
5. Schneider, *Coleridge, Opium and "Kubla Khan,"* 241ff.
6. *Encyclopaedic Dictionary of Religion* (Washington: The Sisters of St. Joseph of Philadelphia and Corpus Publications, 1979), s.v. "Paradise."
7. *NB*, N170 note; *Catalogue of . . . the Bristol Library Society* (Bristol, 1790), 27.
8. Ezekiel 40:1–5, 47:1–12; D. Baly, *The Geography of the Bible*, new ed. (New York: Harper and Row, 1974), 186; J. Milton, *Paradise Lost* 1:411; Revelation 21:8.
9. S. Morinus, *De Paradiso Terrestri*, prefatory essay to S. Bochartus, *Geographia Sacra* (Lugdunum, 1690), 12–13.
10. J. Donne, "Hymne to God my God, in my sicknesse" 21–22.
11. Zechariah 14:8.
12. Dante, *Inferno* (Temple edition, London: Dent, 1932) 34. 110 note.
13. Morinus, *De Paradiso Terrestri*, 12–13.
14. S. Bochartus, *Geographia Sacra* (Lugdunum, 1690), 241, 360, and index s. vv. "Abora," "Chabora."
15. *CL*, 1:205.
16. *Paradise Lost* 4. 214–15.
17. *Paradise Lost* 4. 229–30, 248, 133–39, 172.
18. *Religious Musings* 332.
19. *Paradise Lost* 1. 452–55.

20. J. B. Beer, *Coleridge the Visionary* (London: Chatto and Windus, 1959), 248; G. Yarlott, *Coleridge and the Abyssinian Maid* (London: Methuen, 1967), 141ff.

21. "Nativity Ode" 181–84.

22. *Paradise Lost* 1. 439–41.

23. *Religious Musings* 403.

24. *Ode to the Departing Year* 144.

25. Burnet, *The Sacred Theory of the Earth*, 57; Darwin, *The Botanic Garden* 1. 3. 149–54.

26. Yarlott, *Coleridge and the Abyssinian Maid*, 145.

27. Revelation 4:6.

28. "Dejection: an Ode" 64–65.

29. Johnson's *Dictionary* (1755) and *O.E.D.* s.v. "dome": Pope's *Odyssey* 7. 106; Wordsworth, "Lines written as a School Exercise" 90; Wordsworth, "Composed upon Westminster Bridge" 6 (note plural); Robinson *Poems* 1:227–28; Pope's *Odyssey* 7. 110–21.

30. John 4:13–14; Ezekiel 47:9; Revelation 22:1–3.

31. Piper, "Mount Abora," *Notes and Queries* n.s. 20 (1973): 288–89.

32. Daniel 3:5.

33. J. Shelton, "The Autograph Manuscript of 'Kubla Khan' and an Interpretation," *Review of English Literature* 7 (1966): 32–33.

34. *Religious Musings* 91–93.

35. Revelation 14:6.

36. T. Gray, *The Poems of Gray and Collins*, ed. A. L. Poole (Oxford: Clarendon Press, 1919), 156.

37. "Monody on the Death of Chatterton" 29–31.

38. *Religious Musings* 409–15.

39. M. Bodkin, *Archetypal Patterns in Poetry* (London: Oxford University Press, 1934), 94–95.

40. B. Pascal, *Pensées, in Oeuvres Complètes*, ed. J. Chevalier (Paris: Pleiade, 1962), 1224. (Author's translation.)

Chapter 5. Nature and the Gothic in *Christabel*

1. A. H. Nethercot, *The Road to Tryermaine* (Chicago: University of Chicago Press, 1939), 25.

2. E.g., H. House, *Coleridge* (London: Rupert Hart Davies, 1953), 122–30; R. H. Fogle, *The Idea of Coleridge's Criticism* (Berkeley and Los Angeles: University of California Press, 1962), 130–59; M. Emslie and P. Edwards, "The Limitations of Langsdale," *Essays in Criticism* 20 (1970): 57–70 and "Thoughts all so unlike each other," *English Studies* 52 (1971): 236–46.

3. E. E. Bostetter, *The Romantic Ventriloquists* (Englewood Cliffs, N.J.: Prentice-Hall, 1963), 8.

4. House, *Coleridge*, 130.

5. House, *Coleridge*, 124–25.

6. Emslie and Edwards, "The Limitations of Langsdale," 57.

7. *Christabel* 57–65.

8. J. Adlard, "The Quantock 'Christabel,' " *Philological Quarterly* 50 (1971): 230–38.

9. F. J. Child, *The English and Scottish Popular Ballads* (London: Oxford University Press, 1956), 1:216, 323, 325, 339ff.

10. "Sir Cauline" 34–35 in Percy's *Reliques*, ed. H. B. Wheatley (London: Swann, Sonnerschein, Lowry, 1887), 1:64.

11. "Sir Cauline" 80–89 in Percy's *Reliques*, 1:65.

12. *MC*, 371.

13. Bostetter, *The Romantic Ventriloquists*, 125.
14. *The Destiny of Nations* 253–71.
15. Dorothy Wordsworth, *The Alfoxden Journal* in *The Journals of Dorothy Wordsworth*, ed. William Knight (London: Macmillan, 1892), 17 February; 7, 20, 21, 24, 25, 27 March; 6 April.
16. "Dejection: an Ode" 68.
17. *The Watchman*, 25 March 1796.
18. A. Huxley, *Do What You Will* (New York: Doubleday Doran, 1929), 117.
19. *Tintern Abbey* 39–42.
20. Saint John of the Cross, *Poems*, trans. R. Campbell (London: Penguin, 1960), 99.
21. *King Lear* 4. 6. 206.
22. *Christabel* 457–58, 463–69.
23. *Christabel* 315–22.
24. *Christabel* 438–44.
25. *PW,* 269.
26. "Lines written in the Album at Elbingerode" 17–20 app. crit.
27. "Ode to the Duchess of Devonshire" 74–75.

Chapter 6. Changing Ideas and the "Letter to Asra"

1. *CL,* 2:1189–90.
2. *CL,* 1:209, 284, 147.
3. *CL,* 1:518–19, 676.
4. Orsini, *Coleridge and German Idealism,* 183.
5. Ibid.
6. *Quarterly Review* 66 (1840); 382.
7. *CL,* 2:790.
8. J. O. Hayden, "Coleridge's 'Dejection: an Ode,' " *English Studies* 52 (1971): 133.
9. *CL,* 2:797.
10. House, *Coleridge,* 186.
11. House, *Coleridge,* 166.
12. *CL,* 2:798.
13. Ibid.
14. I. Kant, *Critique of Pure Reason,* trans. J. M. D. Micklejohn (London: Dent, 1934), B 152.
15. Piper, *The Active Universe,* chap. 7 passim.
16. "To William Wordsworth . . ." 61–66.

Chapter 7. Symbolism and the Defense of Religion

1. *NB, N2444, N2447.*
2. *NB, N2448.*
3. *NB, N2546.*
4. J. H. Muirhead, *Coleridge as a Philosopher* (London: Allen and Unwin, 1930); T. McFarland, *Coleridge and the Pantheist Tradition* (Oxford: Clarendon Press, 1969).
5. P. Ward, "Coleridge's Critical Theory of the Symbol," *Texas Studies in Literature and Language* 8 (1966): 32.
6. *CC,* 4. 2:238; *CC* 4. 2:160; *CC* 4. 1:417; *TT,* 26 January 1823; *TT,* 2 June 1824; *MAL,* 249.
7. Orsini, *Coleridge and German Idealism,* 166.

8. *CC*, 4.1:477.

9. *CC*, 4.1:492.

10. *CC*, 4.1:470.

11. *CC*, 4.1:501.

12. Kant, *Critique of Judgement*, trans. J. C. Meredith (Oxford: Clarendon Press, 1964), para. 59.

13. *CC*, 10:20.

14. *BL*, 1:100.

15. Orsini, *Coleridge and German Idealism*, 227.

16. Ibid.

17. F. Schelling, *Ideen zu einer philosophie der Nature* (Leipzig, 1797), 2:6.

18. *Academy Oration Concerning the Relation of the Plastic Arts to Nature*, trans. in Herbert Read, *The True Voice of Feeling* (London: Faber, 1953), 321–64.

19. *BL*, 2:255–59.

20. *BL*, 2:259.

21. Read, *The True Voice of Feeling*, 20.

22. Orsini, *Coleridge and German Idealism*, 37–42.

23. *CC*, 6:30.

24. J. A. Hodgson, "Transcendental Tropes: Coleridge's Rhetoric of Allegory and Symbol," in *Allegory, Myth, Symbol*, ed. M. W. Bloomfield (Cambridge: Harvard University Press, 1981), 277.

25. *AR*, 253.

26. Wellek, *A History of Modern Criticism*, 2:174.

27. J. R. Barth, *The Symbolic Imagination* (Princeton: Princeton University Press, 1977), 9.

28. Abrams, "Coleridge and the Romantic View of the World," in *Coleridge's Variety*, ed. J. H. Beer (London: Macmillan, 1974), 150–51.

29. K. M. Wheeler, *Sources, Processes and Methods in Coleridge's "Biographia Literaria"* (Cambridge: Cambridge University Press, 1980), 141–46, 149.

30. *CC*, 6:78–79.

31. *CL*, 2:861.

32. *CC*, 6:29.

33. Ibid.

34. *CC*, 6:30.

35. *CL*, 1:209, 284, 147.

36. *Psalms* 137:9.

37. *AR*, 74 (quoted by Hodgson in *Allegory, Myth, Symbol*, 274).

Works Cited

Abrams, Meyer H. "Coleridge and the Romantic View of the World." In *Coleridge's Variety,* edited by J. Beer. London: Macmillan, 1974.

———. *Natural Supernaturalism: Tradition and Revolution in Romantic Literature.* New York: W. W. Norton, 1971.

Adlard, John. "The Quantock 'Christabel.'" *Philological Quarterly* 50 (1971): 230–38.

Akenside, Mark. *The Poetical Works of M. Akenside.* Edited by G. Gilfillan. Edinburgh: James Nichol, 1857.

Auden, W. H. *The Enchafed Flood; or the Romantic Iconography of the Sea.* London: Faber, 1951.

Baly, Denis. *The Geography of the Bible.* New edition. New York: Harper and Row, 1974.

Barth, J. Robert. *Coleridge and Christian Doctrine.* Cambridge: Harvard University Press, 1969.

———. *The Symbolic Imagination.* Princeton: Princeton University Press, 1977.

Bate, Walter J. *Coleridge.* New York: Macmillan, 1968.

Beer, John B. "Coleridge and Boehme's 'Aurora.'" *Notes and Queries,* n.s. 10 (1963): 183–84.

———. *Coleridge the Visionary.* London: Chatto and Windus, 1959.

Belsham, Thomas. *Memoirs of the Reverend Theophilus Lindsey including . . . a General View of the Progress of Unitarian Doctrine in England and America.* London, 1812.

Bochartus, Samuel. *Geographia Sacra.* Lugdunum, 1690.

Bodkin, Maud. *Archetypal Patterns in Poetry: Psychological Studies in Imagination.* London: Oxford University Press, 1934.

Bostetter, Edward E. *The Romantic Ventriloquists.* Englewood Cliffs, N.J.: Prentice-Hall, 1963.

Brett, Raymond L. "Coleridge's Theory of Imagination." *Essays and Studies,* n.s. 2 (1949): 75–90.

Bristol Library Society. *Catalogue of the Books belonging to the Bristol Library Society.* Bristol, 1790.

Burnet, Thomas. *The Sacred Theory of the Earth.* 2nd ed. London, 1691.

Chambers, Edmund K. *Samuel Taylor Coleridge: a Biographical Study.* Oxford: Clarendon Press, 1938.

Child, Francis J. *The English and Scottish Popular Ballads.* 5 vols. London: Oxford University Press, 1956.

Coleridge, Henry N. "Review of the Honorable Mrs Norton, Miss Barrett [and others]." *The Quarterly Review* 66 (1840): 374–418.

Dante, Alighieri. *The Temple Classics: The Inferno of Dante Alighieri.* London: Dent, 1932.

———. *The Temple Classics: The Purgatorio of Dante Alighieri.* London: Dent, 1937.

Darwin, Erasmus. *The Botanic Garden: a Poem in Two Parts . . . with philosophical notes.* London, 1791.

De Quincey, Thomas. *Collected Writings.* Edited by D. Masson. 14 vols. Edinburgh: P. and C. Black, 1889–90.

Donne, John. *The Poems of John Donne.* Edited by H. J. C. Grierson. London: Oxford University Press, 1912.

Empson, William, and David Pirie, eds. *Coleridge's Verse: a Selection.* London: Faber, 1972.

Emslie, Macdonald, and Paul Edwards. "The Limitations of Langsdale: a Reading of 'Christabel.'" *Essays in Criticism* 20 (1970): 57–70.

———. "'Thoughts all so unlike each other': the paradoxical in 'Christabel.'" *English Studies* 52 (1971): 236–46.

Encyclopaedic Dictionary of Religion. Washington: The Sisters of Saint Joseph of Philadelphia and Corpus Publications, 1979.

Erdman, David V. "Unrecorded Coleridge Variants." *Studies in Bibliography* 11 (1958): 143–62.

Euripides. *Bacchae.* Edited by D. Cruikshank. Oxford: Clarendon Press, 1941.

Everest, Kelvin. *Coleridge's Secret Ministry: the Context of the Conversation Poems of 1795–8.* Hassocks: Harvester, 1979.

Fogle, Richard H. *The Idea of Coleridge's Criticism.* Berkeley and Los Angeles: University of California Press, 1962.

Forstner, Lorne J. "Coleridge's 'The Ancient Mariner' and the Case for Justifiable Mythocide: an Argument on Psychological, Epistemological and Formal Grounds." *Criticism* 18 (1976): 211–29.

Frei, Hans W. *The Eclipse of Biblical Narrative.* New Haven: Yale University Press, 1974.

Fruman, Norman. *Coleridge the Damaged Archangel.* New York: G. Braziller, 1972.

Garnham, Robert E. *A Sermon preached in the Chapel of Trinity College Cambridge . . . on December 19, 1793*. Cambridge, 1794.

Gerard, Albert S. *English Romantic Poetry: Ethos, Structure and Symbol in Coleridge, Wordsworth, Shelley and Keats*. Berkeley and Los Angeles: University of California Press, 1968.

Gray, Thomas. *The Poems of Gray and Collins*. Edited by A. L. Poole. Oxford: Clarendon Press, 1919.

Griffiths, Olive M. *Religion and Learning: a Study of English Presbyterian Thought from the Bartholemew Ejections (1662) to the Foundation of the Unitarian Movement*. Cambridge: Cambridge University Press, 1935.

Hayden, John O. "Coleridge's 'Dejection: an Ode.'" *English Studies* 52 (1971) 132–36.

Hazlitt, William. *Works*. Edited by P. P. Howe. 21 vols. London: Dent, 1930–34.

Hegel, Georg W. F. *Saemtliche Werke*. 26 vols. Stuttgart: Frommann, 1956–59.

Hobbes, Thomas. *Leviathan*. Edited by J. S. Thornton. Oxford: Clarendon Press, 1881.

Hodgson, John A. "Transcendental Tropes: Coleridge's Rhetoric of Allegory and Symbol." In *Allegory, Myth, Symbol*, edited by M. W. Bloomfield. Cambridge: Harvard University Press, 1981.

Holt, Raymond V. *The Unitarian Contribution to Social Progress in England*. London: Lindsey, 1952.

House, Humphry. *Coleridge: the Clark Lectures for 1951–2*. London: Rupert Hart Davies, 1953.

Huxley, Aldous. *Do What You Will*. New York: Doubleday Doran, 1929.

Jacobus, Mary. "William Huntingdon's 'Spiritual Sea-voyage': Another Source for 'The Ancient Mariner.'" *Notes and Queries* n.s. 16 (1969) 409–12.

James, David G. *The Romantic Comedy*. London: Oxford University Press, 1948.

Jaspers, David. *Coleridge as Poet and Religious Thinker: Inspiration and Revelation*. London: Macmillan, 1985.

John of the Cross, Saint. *Poems*. Translated by Roy Campbell. London: Penguin, 1960.

Johnson, Samuel. *A Dictionary of the English Language*. London, 1755.

Kant, Immanuel. *Critique of Judgement*. Translated by J. C. Meredith. Oxford: Clarendon Press, 1964.

———. *Critique of Pure Reason*. Translated by J. M. D. Micklejohn. London: Dent, 1934.

Lamb, Charles and Mary Lamb. *The Letters of Charles and Mary Lamb*. Edited by E. W. Marrs. Ithaca: Cornell University Press, 1975.

Lawrence, D. H. *Apocalypse*. London: Martin Secker, 1932.

McFarland, Thomas. *Coleridge and the Pantheist Tradition.* Oxford: Clarendon Press, 1969.

McLachlan, Herbert. *The Religious Opinions of Milton, Newton and Locke.* Manchester: Manchester University Press, 1934.

———. *The Unitarian Movement in the Religious Life of England: Its Contribution to Thought and Learning, 1700–1900.* London: Allen and Unwin, 1934.

Marcel, Gabriel. *Coleridge et Schelling.* Paris: Aubier Montaigne, 1971.

Martin, Charles G. "Coleridge and Cudworth: a Source for 'The Eolian Harp.'" *Notes and Queries* n.s. 13 (1966) 173.

Matheson, Ann. "The Influence of Cowper's 'The Task' on Coleridge's Conversation Poems." In *New Approaches to Coleridge,* edited by Donald S. Sultana. London: Vision Press, 1981, 137–50.

Milton, John. *Poetical Works.* Edited by H. Darbishire. London: Oxford University Press, 1958.

Moorman, Mary. *William Wordsworth, A Biography: The Early Years, 1770–1803.* London: Oxford University Press, 1957.

Morinus, Stephanus. *De Paradiso Terrestri.* Prefatory essay to S. Bochartus, *Geographia Sacra.* Lugdunum, 1690.

Muirhead, John H. *Coleridge as a Philosopher.* London: Allen and Unwin, 1920.

Nethercote, Arthur H. *The Road to Tryermaine: a Study of the History, Background and Purposes of Coleridge's "Christabel."* Chicago: University of Chicago Press, 1939.

Newton, Isaac. *Opera.* Edited by S. Horsley. 5 vols. London, 1779–85.

Orsini, Gian N. G. *Coleridge and German Idealism.* Carbondale: Southern Illinois University Press, 1969.

Pascal, Blaise. *Oeuvres Complètes.* Edited by J. Chevalier. Paris: Pléiade, 1962.

Percy, Thomas. *Reliques of Ancient English Poetry.* Edited by H. B. Wheatley. 3 vols. London: Swann, Sonnenschein, Lowry, 1885.

Piper, Herbert W. *The Active Universe: Pantheism and the Concept of Imagination in the English Romantic Poets.* London: Athlone, 1962.

———. "Coleridge's Note on Unitarianism, Orthodoxy and Atheism." *Notes and Queries,* n.s. 25 (1978): 220–21.

———. "Mount Abora." *Notes and Queries,* n.s. 20 (1973): 286–89.

———. "Shakespeare's 'Antony and Cleopatra' V ii 279–81." *Explicator* 26 (1967): 10.

Pope, Alexander. *The Odyssey of Homer.* London: Oxford University Press, 1906.

Potter, Stephen. *Coleridge and STC.* London: Jonathan Cape, 1935.

Priestley, Joseph. *The Conclusion of . . . Dr Hartley's Observations . . . illustrated in the events of the present times, with notes.* London, 1794.

———. *Disquisitions relating to Matter and Spirit: to which is added the philosophical doctrine concerning the origin of the soul and the nature of matter.* London, 1777.

———. *The Present State of Europe compared with Antient Prophecies: a sermon . . . on leaving England.* London, 1794.

———. *Theological and Miscellaneous Works.* Edited by J. T. Rutt. 20 vols. London, 1817.

Purchas, Samuel. *Hakluytus Posthumus; or Purchas his Pilgrimes.* London, 1625.

———. *Purchas his Pilgrimage: or, Relations of the World and the Religions observed in all ages.* London, 1613.

Randell, Fred V. "Coleridge and the Contentiousness of Romantic Nightingales." *Studies in Romanticism* 21 (1982): 33–55.

Read, Herbert. *The True Voice of Feeling: Studies in Romantic Poetry.* London: Faber, 1953.

Robinson, Mary. *Poems.* 2 vols. London, 1803.

Schelling, Friedrich W. J. v. "Academy Oration concerning the relation of the Plastic Arts to Nature." Translated in H. Read, *The True Voice of Feeling: Studies in Romantic Poetry.* London: Faber, 1953.

———. *Ideen zu einer Philosophie der Nature.* Leipzig, 1797.

Schneider, Elisabeth W. *Coleridge, "Opium and Kubla Khan."* Chicago: University of Chicago Press, 1966.

Shelton, John. "The Autograph Manuscript of 'Kubla Khan' and an Interpretation." *Review of English Literature* 7 (1966): 32–42.

Schrickx, W. "Coleridge and the Cambridge Platonists." *Review of English Literature* 7 (1966): 71–91.

Ward, Patricia. "Coleridge's Theory of the Symbol." *Texas Studies in Literature and Language* 8 (1966): 15–32.

Wasserman, Earl R. "The English Romantics: the grounds of knowledge." *Studies in Romanticism* 4 (1964): 17–34.

Wellek, René. *A History of Modern Criticism, 1750–1950.* 4 vols. New Haven: Yale University Press, 1955–65.

Wheeler, Katherine M. *The Creative Mind in Coleridge's Poetry.* London: Heinemann, 1981.

———. *Sources, Processes and Methods in Coleridge's "Biographia Literaria."* Cambridge: Cambridge University Press, 1980.

Willey, Basil. *The Eighteenth Century Background: Studies on the Idea of Nature in the Thought of the Period.* London: Chatto and Windus, 1946.

———. *Samuel Taylor Coleridge.* London: Chatto and Windus, 1972.

Wimsatt, William K. *The Verbal Icon.* New York: Noonday, 1958.

Wordsworth, D. *The Journals of Dorothy Wordsworth.* Edited by William Knight. Vol. 1. London: Macmillan, 1892.

Wordsworth, William. *The Poetical Works of Wordsworth.* Edited by T. Hutchinson. London: Oxford University Press, 1912.

Yarlott, Geoffrey. *Coleridge and the Abyssinian Maid.* London: Methuen, 1967.

Yeats, William B. *Selected Prose.* Edited by A. N. Jeffares. London: Macmillan, 1964.

Young, Edward. *Night Thoughts.* Edited by G. Gilfillan. Edinburgh: James Nichol, 1853.

Index